C.H.U.R.C.H. Girls
Stories of Victory, Success, & Triumph

A Compilation Presented by
Tequita C. Brice

C.H.U.R.C.H. Girls: Stories of Victory, Success, & Triumph
Copyright © 2018 Tequita C. Brice

All rights reserved. No part of this book may be reproduced, distributed or transmitted in any form by any means, graphics, electronics. Or mechanical, including photocopy, recording, taping, or by any information storage or retrieval system, without permission in writing from the publisher, except in the case of reprints in the context of reviews, quotes, or references.

Scripture quotations marked "KJV" or unmarked are taken from the Holy Bible, King James Version, Cambridge, 1769. Used by permission. All rights reserved.

Unless otherwise indicated, all Scripture quotations are taken from THE MESSAGE, copyright © 1993, 1994, 1995, 1996, 2000, 2001, 2002 by Eugene H. Peterson. Used by permission of NavPress. All rights reserved. Represented by Tyndale House Publishers, Inc.

Scripture quotations marked "NIV" are taken from the Holy Bible, New International Version ®, Copyright © 1973, 1978, 1984 by International Bible Society. Used by permission of Zondervan Publishing House. All rights reserved.

Scripture quotations marked "NLT" are taken from the Holy Bible, New Living Translation, copyright ©1996, 2004, 2007, 2013, 2015 by Tyndale House Foundation. Used by permission

of Tyndale House Publishers, Inc., Carol Stream, Illinois 60188.
All rights reserved.

Published by WriteIt2Life Publishing;
a division of The L.I.F.E Group, Inc.
P.O. Box 619 Trinity, NC 27370
336.701.2083 | www.icoach2life.com

Cover Design | Allison Arnett www.branditbeautifully.com
Editing & Proofreading | Tamika Sims www.inkpendiva.com

Printed by IngramSpark
Printed in the United States of America

ISBN: 0998784458
ISBN-13: 978-0-9987844-5-8

Dedication

This book is dedicated to all the women who have modeled lives of godliness and holiness before me and have made me proud to claim the name of Jesus Christ.

I am a C.H.U.R.C.H. Girl, it is plain to see.
I am a C.H.U.R.C.H. Girl – unapologetically.

TABLE OF CONTENTS

Foreword xi

Introduction 13

Ten Minute Relationships 17
    Paula Y. Obie

God's Favorite 31
    Harriet Grimes

I Sing Because I'm Happy 43
    Sheryl Yelverton

I Once was Blind, but Now I See 55
    Sandra McCullough

Resilience Is My Portion 67
    Kendra Diggs

Reflection of Reality 77
    Lakesha Holiday

Resilience through Relationship 89
    Kareen Hartley

Broken to be Made Whole 101
    Shauntia Stanback

He Fashioned Me Classy 113
    Tracey R. Wolfe

You Can't Take My Oil 125
    Cassandra Elliott

With His Stripes I Am Healed 137
    Alberta Gail Wright

This is my Story, This is my Song 149
    Robin V. Yelverton

About the Visionary 161

Connect With Us 164

FOREWORD

I am thrilled to be writing this foreword on such a timely, inspiring book that highlights with transparency the ups and downs of the lives of Chosen, Holy, Unique, Resilient, Classy, and Healed women.

First of all, I would like to commend the visionary, Tequita C. Brice, on her creativity and idea of bringing these testimonials to life. I have known Tequita since she was a child, and she comes from a great legacy of gifted women. I can say like the Apostle Paul when he was encouraging his spiritual son, Timothy, *"You have come from a grandmother, and a mother who had unfeigned faith, stir up the gift within you."* Truly the gift of God has been stirred, as we read the pages of an awesome compilation of stories of hardship to triumph.

This book, *C.H.U.R.C.H. Girls: Stories of Victory, Success & Triumph* is distinguished by the heart of women sharing their truths whose foundation is church, yet they opened their lives to show that their experiences are tangible, relatable, life lessons for all who read them. You will be inspired, encouraged, and empowered.

Tracey Troy
Pastor of Victory in Jesus Ministries

Introduction

Every woman has a story. The narrative of a "C.H.U.R.C.H. Girl" is that she is different, however, to a world that doesn't understand, the different is not always perceived as a *good*. C.H.U.R.C.H. Girls is a compilation of stories of the victory, triumph, and success of extraordinary women just like you who dispel the negative stigma of what a C.H.U.R.C.H. Girl is and celebrate the honor it is to wear the crown.

C.H.U.R.C.H. Girls are precious. C.H.U.R.C.H. Girls aren't just special, they are distinctive. 2 Corinthians 4:7-12 (MSG) sums up why,

> *"If you only look at us, you might well miss the brightness. We carry this precious Message around in the unadorned clay pots of our ordinary lives. That's to prevent anyone from confusing God's incomparable power with us. As it is, there's not much chance of that. You know for yourselves that we're not much to look at. We've been surrounded and battered by troubles, but we're not*

demoralized; we're not sure what to do, but we know that God knows what to do; we've been spiritually terrorized, but God hasn't left our side; we've been thrown down, but we haven't broken. What they did to Jesus, they do to us—trial and torture, mockery and murder; what Jesus did among them, he does in us—he lives! Our lives are at constant risk for Jesus' sake, which makes Jesus' life all the more evident in us. While we're going through the worst, you're getting in on the best!"

In *C.H.U.R.C.H. Girls*, twelve women share their stories of victory, success, and triumph with you as a witness that they are overcome by the blood of the Lamb and the word of their testimony. They share that falling doesn't mean failure and that they have had the courage to get back up and try it again.

This project was birthed out a desire to share with the world, the treasure that C.H.U.R.C.H. Girls possess that makes us so valuable. We are valuable because we are **C**hosen, **H**oly, **U**nique, **R**esilient, **C**lassy, and **H**ealed. We were Chosen in Christ before the foundation of the world, we are Holy, sanctified, and set apart, we are Unique because we have been bought with a price, we are Resilient because we have the power to bounce back from any situation life throws our way, we are Classy because we are fearfully and wonderfully made and we are Healed because of the blood of the Lamb!

Chosen, Holy, Unique, Resilient, Classy, and Healed are the

Introduction

characteristics of women whose lives exemplify the benefits of a rich relationship with Christ. It is my prayer that you are inspired, uplifted, and empowered to live your life unapologetically as a C.H.U.R.C.H. Girl.

Tequita

Ten Minute Relationships

Paula Y. Obie

Staring down at my rose gold iPhone, the major mode of all of my interactions and communications, I recall when I was a young girl one of my favorite pastimes was talking to my friends on the telephone. It was so much fun. We would giggle over the silliest things and chat about what happened in school that day for what seemed like hours on end. Being the only girl in a house full of boys, I could talk as long as I wanted. Then, in a moment, that privilege just faded away. Pain, tragedy, and loss shifted my reality from one of happiness and joy to misery.

My home environment remained pastoral however, we now had new leadership along with a new address that came equipped with one phone in the kitchen and one in the master bedroom. Now all phone calls were scrutinized and could only be a total of ten minutes. I always knew someone else was listening on the other line and if I went over my ten minutes, then of course *the voice* would chime in and tell me my time was up. Can you imagine the questions from my friends on next day at school? Word traveled fast about how I was not accessible, how the situation was handled, and they shared what they had witnessed firsthand with others. It was an embarrassing and hurtful reality, for sure.

My entire social life consisted of the following: once or twice a month ten-minute phone calls, hanging out with my friends in school for a little while during or in between classes, or on the bus ride back and forth to and from school, and oh yeah, of course, I would also get to spend a little time with them after church. We were a long-distance pastoral family, so we traveled at least one hour one way each Sunday to our church. If we were lucky, on one of the parishioner visits, we could interact longer and have more than about fifteen minutes — maybe thirty minutes or an hour depending on the nature of the after-church visitations. My brothers and I always joked that we never got to see the end of the Walt Disney Specials because just when we were mesmerized with the storyline, we would hear the words, "We are ready to leave now!" As a matter of fact, I was an adult before I saw the end of the Sunday Walt Disney stories and I have since watched them repeatedly, WITHOUT interruptions on demand.

The result of the ten minute scrutinized calls was a learned behavior that became a forced skill of getting to know people quickly and I began to base major life decisions from being around them for a small amount of time. This became my new normal way of living. Ten minute relationships metaphorically give you very little opportunity to get to the heart of the matter to even decipher if the person is telling you the truth. There was no opportunity for deep thinking or even to ponder and return to the subject and ponder a little more. There was no time, as demonstrated by other households, for my parents to meet the other parents and for us to be together in several scenarios that were outside of the church walls where real conversations and observations could be held. The new mode of relationship building that I was forced to embrace was a shallow type of interaction that resulted in me having devasting friendships and relationships. After a few ten minute interactions, I thought we were OK enough for me to share my heart and my life. One person maybe talked a few minutes and the other a few minutes, and even if you felt the urge to argue a point or start an even deeper level of conversation that required another level of thinking or a challenge, it was time to hang up the phone or end the interaction. As a result, there were many spur of the moment decisions made that formed the basis of me trying to do grown-up things.

As I reflect on that time of maturing, I realize that there was very little emotional or mental maturity required for these interactions. Basically, there was just a lot of time for hiding. It was also simultaneously during this time in my life where I also longed to connect with others socially as I was moving from my teenage years and into my young adult years and my own isolated reality caused me to feel stifled and neglected. This sense of longing and neediness sent out an invisible message that said, *"come hang out with me, I am naïve and in need of any kind of company and am accepting of all,"* and since I wanted and needed so much attention — well, who doesn't need more than ten minutes of attention, I just accepted whatever I could glean from those short timed interactions. This type of mindset created a social foundation of me not understanding the importance of knowing how to have real, sincere, healthy relationships and friendships which caused the disappointments to occur on a regular basis. This way of living and mentality and messaging also resulted in me almost losing my life with the very first boyfriend I ever had. I am now, once again, staring down at the rose gold iPhone as I gaze back at the memory of how God delivered me from that near fatal situation.

Yes, I only had a few interactions with him before we were girlfriend and boyfriend and, of course, I was head over heels in love in a flash. We had been together for about two years, with one of those years being long distance. We had both quit college, moved back to our hometown, and went to work for the same employer as it was one of the easiest places to get a job right out of high school or without a degree. He worked first shift and I worked second shift. This obscure schedule presented a lot of time for activities to take place without my knowledge.

During one night of entertaining, I walked into the kitchen to learn that his drug and alcohol habit had led him to becoming a full blown drug dealer. I was still so naïve to this world, and he took advantage of my inability to understand what was going on. I even went for a ride with him one night and stopped at a friend's house, not knowing the type of transaction that was taking place around me. It was just not my world and he was great at disguising it as one of his many social calls.

On a Friday evening when his friends were over and I stood up to change the channel on the TV, I saw the evidence right in front of me. One of my neighbors who was also visiting, stated quietly, "*You know if we get busted, we are all going to jail. What are you going to do?*" With that bit of information burning inside me, on my next day off from work, I discreetly arranged to move out of our living quarters and into a safe place with family. I was too ashamed to speak of the reasons for needing to move in with my family, so I stated that it was simply for financial reasons.

Following the move, I was asked to work my second shift

and a few hours on third shift as the person was sick and could not come to work. When I went into the breakroom during my break time, a lady who knew my family, began asking questions that did not make sense to me. Then she began sharing her own interactions as well. The statement that got my attention, though was, *"I saw his car in the parking lot when I came in. It was parked beside yours. I thought you all had broken up!"* Fearing the worst, I decided to work the entire shift and not go home until 7 a.m. When I walked past him as he was coming in for his shift he remarked, *"So, you decided to work all night long,"* which was another red flag.

It was the next evening that I walked out to my car, when his car was parked next to mine that he spoke of and pointed to a bag with a weapon he was planning to use the night before, however, my decision to work late caused him to do some deep thinking and change his mind. I recognized the weapon bag and knew that it had his pistol inside. The situation might have further escalated, however, the family friend recommended that I not walk out by myself and from that point forward there was someone around to make sure my car cranked and that I drove safely home. I drove away wondering how my life had turned into such a dangerous mess and I had no idea how in the world it got that way.

Shortly thereafter I changed jobs, living locations, and phone numbers. I do wish I could say that it was a lesson learned, however, I would be lying to you if I did. Since then, I have been in yet more than one dangerous situation that could have ended my life. What's more, I just didn't get why I was this magnet for trouble. What in the world was wrong? It wasn't until a few decades later that I could even draw the correlation between why I did not take the time to learn the truth about people and why I was so desperate for companionship and friendship that I risked integrity, credibility, and truth. I am, and I repeat, I am only here by the Grace of Almighty God as this was only the first of two times when someone decided that my life was theirs to take, just because. Just as God would not allow me to suffer from a pistol, He had to intervene a second time. This time, He sent an angel to keep the knife from pushing through my belt and hitting my vital organs. Again, this was another type of relationship that was a whirlwind romance with no time to stop and count the costs, review the risks, and adhere to sound counsel about whether or not I should proceed forward. I asked God, *"Am I too willing to overlook the truth?"* With seemingly no answers coming, I had no choice but to embrace the fact that I have been chosen – favored by God for something greater than I probably have even imagined.

I am, once again, staring at my rose gold iPhone as I think about how God was watching over me and my life even as I lived so casually. The ten minute relationship building technique also impacted how my family relationships were built. We did not spend any time bonding together. We were separated most of the time and interacted very little. The interactions we did have were mostly one-way monologs that became strained very quickly. Most of the time the conversations were over-controlling with only two or three topics discussed. I often wondered as Christians, people who supposedly knew God best, how we did not understand or embrace the importance of spending quality time getting to know each other and getting to see them in several scenarios before we started making major life choices with them. Because of this behavior, the outcome of most of my relationships resulted in disappointing, devastating outcomes that left me feeling desperate and insecure.

I also reflect on the lives of my siblings and their liaisons. Again, because we all practiced the same social skills, I could see the common thread that rippled throughout all of our lives. I was really invested in figuring us out so, I took out a piece of post-it poster paper, placed our names on each one, and placed them on the wall. Then I listed our names at the top divided the paper into two sections for each sibling with a heading that read, **Healthy Relationships** and **Unhealthy Relationships**. After writing down the data for each of us, I sat back and read the listings. The revelations were clear. Yes, we are anointed, royal priesthoods, and loooooooove God with all of our hearts. We stayed in church day and night, preached, taught, prayed, ministered in song and in spoken word, but the results of our interactions with others, especially those personal relationships as well as those covenant relationships revealed commonalities that caused me to sit with tears streaming down my face.

The questions I asked at that time are the ones I still ask now: How could I get involved with someone who did not have a problem abusing me verbally, emotionally and physically? How could I continue to connect myself with someone who did not even understand the importance of working and paying for the things that cause us to be grown-ups? How could I believe the lies when someone said, "*Sure, we can do that*" and then when the time came to deliver, they were nowhere to be found? How did I survive the impact of the decisions others made for me that caused me to blindly go along with as if I had no mind of my own? How did I survive the two attempts to end my life? How did I survive sitting in the dark because someone did not want to pay the light bill, but always had enough money to purchase something for themselves? How did I survive the con games that resulted in me signing papers and going along with a plan that I later became totally financially responsible for that destroyed my own financial worthiness?

Were these questions that I could also apply to many of my own family members? Absolutely! The commonality was the application of the social behaviors that did not allow us to focus or embrace building any type of meaningful, ethical, relationship based on the real values, or have real dreams with a plan for how we could work together to accomplish them. If I couldn't trust you, then why was I with you? If you are disrespectful then why am I with you? If you steal from me (oh, I mean, borrow money, say you are going to pay it back and do not) then why would I think we could have anything of considerable value together?

I wrote next to the names of the folks on my post-it sheet the losses (red marker) and the gains (green markers) that I received while maintaining these associations. Yes, it was really an eye-opening experience for me. After entering the information about myself, I did not have the energy to apply the details to my family member's post-it notes. This was an arduous, but important lesson for me. What we needed was wisdom, above all things. . . wisdom that could only come from one source and that source was God!

Right now, I am, yet again, starring at this beautiful rose-gold colored iPhone that allows me to connect with any of my contacts in a number of ways and I can talk to them as long as I desire. I am stopping, once again, to ponder over the years, and to question how I would rate myself on a scale of 1 to 5 on the social technique of getting to know others well enough to determine if we should be at least friends? The answer is, I am not sure my techniques have really improved at all, not really. These reflections now cause me to also ponder how I learned to have a real relationship with God. As a child, I knew how to celebrate and worship, but it was many, many years before I realized that my relationship with God had to be based upon a lot more than just short visits. For example, I learned at a very early age how to pray; however it was many, many years before my prayer life turned into a daily time spent with a God who loved me more than anything that I could imagine. It is clear that spending daily time with God has transformed me in so many areas of my life. I have learned from professional liaisons how to communicate with people who do not look like me. Through taking the time to spend with God, on a regular basis, I am able to mirror the importance of using that same technique to get to know others. I have not completely mastered the technique however, I follow the same rules that I apply to keeping my relationship with God: I speak, I listen intently, and I observe the behaviors. It seems to be working.

ABOUT PAULA

Paula Y. Obie is a native of Orange and Durham counties and the daughter of Elder Samuel B. Obie and the late Rev. Joyce Long Obie and Elder Catherine P. Obie. Paula gave her life to Christ at a young age and since proclaiming Christ, she has faced many obstacles but held on to the scripture in 1 John 4:4 (KJV) *". . . greater is He that is in you than he that is in the world."* A major life altering event, the passing of her Mama Joyce, propelled her into the role of caretaker. It was during this traumatic life change that Paula learned the importance of using written and oral communication; however, the environment in which she lived forced her gift of writing to become dominant. It was the gift of writing that helped usher in God's healing and deliverance and unveiled her teaching and training ministries.

Paula graduated from Southern High School with Academic Honors in 1978 and in 2009 completed her Bachelor's degree in

Business Management and obtained a Master's in Project Management in 2012. Dr. Obie is in the final stages of completing her Doctorate degree in Organization Development and Change at Colorado Technical University.

Paula is the epitome of a C(Chosen), H(Holy), U(Unique), R(Resilient),C(Classy), H(Healed) girl and has embraced each life scenario as God's platform to prepare her for the next stage of His plan for her life. Her professional career includes training and development, human resource management, and an independent beauty consultant. Paula is a member of Monument of Faith Ministries, Eden, NC under the leadership of Elder Lannie Robertson.

Connect with Paula at www.facebook.com/paula.obie

GOD'S FAVORITE

Harriet Grimes

Fr as long as I can remember I've always known I was chosen; hand-picked, selected by God, His favorite. I remember feeling the presence of God around me from as early as age ten. I was in the house with my mom and I asked her *"Why am I feeling chills on my head and neck but I'm not cold?"* She looked at me, smiled, and said, *"You're being anointed by God!"* I was confused because I had heard of God's anointing but honestly never thought it applied to little old me. I asked her, *"What am I being anointed for?"* To that she replied, *"I don't know but I believe God has chosen you for something great."* I'm sure there was a sounder theological explanation for what I was actually experiencing, however, for the purposes of that moment in my life, my mother's explanation sufficed.

Throughout my life I've always remembered that day, the day God decided to make me aware that I had a greater purpose, that there was something special about me. I used to want to fit in with everyone and be just like my friends but as soon as I tried to be like them, God would remind me that I was different and no matter how much I tried to fit in, I wouldn't because I was special. Consequently, though, He has always had his hand on me keeping me from all manner of danger even when I was too silly to be aware of what was going on around me. I tried so hard to fit in that at twenty-one years old, I entered into a downward spiral from which I didn't know if I would be able to recover.

I had just ended a three year relationship with my first boyfriend. I had convinced myself while I was with him that I, alone, could force our relationship to work. So, after ending the relationship I felt lost. I felt as if I had no identity anymore. Everyone associated me with him and it reminded me that I failed at making this work. In hind sight, I realize that in all things working together for my good, the relationship had purpose and connected me with forces and invaluable people I still have in my corner to this day. I was so lost, though, that I felt running to another city would change everything for me. It did change everything, just not in the way I thought.

So I didn't have to go it alone, one of my sister's decided to move with me. We made the hour and a half trek from

Greensboro to Charlotte in hopes of beginning a new life. I was tired of being quiet, shy, and "looking the part" all of the time, so I decided to reinvent myself. In my head I proclaimed, *"I will now be a new person."* I thought no one there knew me so what did I have to lose. The new city and new found job afforded me the opportunity to meet new people. I began to connect with different men and in connecting I mean engaging in ominous sexual relationships with anybody I wanted to. I knew I was playing a dangerous game with my life but still hurting and broken, I no longer cared about the consequences. I was out of control and there was no stopping me. There were weeks I drank, partied, and clubbed six days a week. The only day I didn't was Sunday, go figure but I had completely lost myself. All I wanted to do was be "normal" like everybody else that was out. I was trying hard to numb my pain but everything still hurt.

One Sunday, after taking a "break" from partying I thought, *"Maybe I'll go back to church."* So, I visited a church that was very similar to one I grew up in. As I sat in the back pew I felt awkward, ashamed, and lower than I'd ever felt before. I couldn't figure out how I'd gotten to this point. How had I strayed so far away from my roots? As I sobbed, the devil crept into my mind and convinced me I should leave because everyone was looking at me and could see my shame. Convicted and confused, I ran out of the service and tried to get myself together. I started thinking, *"Maybe I should just settle down with one guy?"* After running around with multiple guys for months, I decided I was going choose one lucky guy.

I chose one... unfortunately, one that already had a family. Before you call me home wrecker, cradle robber, and any other name you may be thinking of, remember I was broken and hurting. My rationale was not rational at all. I thought I could convince him to leave, so I did whatever he asked me to do. I began writing bad checks for him, cashing random checks, spending the money with him, smoking, drinking, sleeping with him and continuing to live completely reckless. During this time, God was the farthest thing from my mind. I just wanted this man to love me and nothing else mattered.

As the relationship progressed, we started to argue a lot and things weren't so perfect anymore. One day, hanging out with his friend, we ended up in another argument. I got out of his truck slamming the door behind me. Before I knew it, he ran over to the other ride of the truck, grabbed me by my neck and lifted me up in the air. I don't remember what he said but I do remember everything around me going dark. When I regained consciousness, I recall the look of complete and utter shock on his friend's face. He let me go and got back in the truck. I got back in as well and he drove me home. No one said a word but at that moment I was seeing red. All I could think about was how I was going to kill him! I didn't sleep that night at all. Constant thoughts of how I was going to get him back ran through my mind. No one had ever laid their hands on me. I wanted him dead and I plotted to do just that.

The next day, I invited him over. I knew after the day before, he would be suspicious of me wanting to see how the rest of our relationship would play out because we'd never had that kind of exchange before. I managed to convince him that all was well. He thought he was coming over for a booty call but I had other plans in mind. Before he knew what was happening, I had him handcuffed to the chair with a knife to his neck. Yes, I had lost my mind! He was crying and pleading with me to let him go. Over and over he kept saying how sorry he was and that he would never do it again. I was standing in front of him frozen with the knife pointed at him. At some point, I zoned him completely out and although he was yelling and pleading right in front of me, he began to sound distant like he was a million miles away. My own thoughts of hurt and anguish started to mix with another voice in my head, *"This is not right, you need to let him go. You're better than this. Put the knife down and let him go."* For what seemed like a lifetime, I paced back and forth with everything going through my mind. I fought the words of reason trying to bring me back as hard as I could but eventually, all it took was that one instant for God to show himself and remind me that I was his. I began to hear clearly that if no one else loved me, he did.

I finally uncuffed him and told him to get out. Exhausted, I went to my bedroom and cried. I got down on my knees and prayed. I needed this soul tie to be broken and I knew only God could do it. I could not be connected to any more volatile situations. It was my first time praying in a very long time and in a short time I felt the room being filled with his presence.

You would have thought being handcuffed to a chair with a knife at his throat would have been enough for him to leave me alone – Not so! Even when I refused to see or talk to him anymore. Initially, I had the strength to ignore his calls. Then, one day his friend approached me, told me how much he missed me and that he really needed to talk. All I could think was, *"I'm trying to get back on track with the Lord and he's a distraction."* However, I wasn't strong enough to resist. I agreed to meet him at his friend's house. I thought after not seeing him for weeks, I wouldn't want to be with him. I was so wrong. I saw him and wanted him all over again.

We sat and talked with each other and it was like when we first met. One thing led to another and we ended up in bed together again. For the next two weeks I ignored him and tried to keep him out of my mind. I knew I had really messed up. I just prayed and asked God to please save me and I promised to never do this again. Then my menstrual cycle was abnormal. It started and the same day it stopped. I was a nervous wreck. I ran to the store and bought three different early detect pregnancy tests. The results for all three were positive. I passed out on my bathroom floor. *"This can't be happening to me!"*

I hated myself for falling, being weak and allowing myself to get used. I cried constantly and refused to tell anyone but I had to tell him. As devastated as I was, he was excited. I wanted to end the pregnancy but he wanted to keep it. I knew I could not be connected to this man forever. I became distant and stopped talking to my sisters. I was irritable, broken, and still hurting. I was majorly off task and had no idea how to get back.

You have to understand that the devil doesn't want you to fulfill God's promise for your life. There will always be obstacles, traps, and stumbling blocks to throw you off task. In the weeks that followed, I experienced more of the same volatile and disrespectful behavior. I made a decision to end the pregnancy. I started praying again and God began to deal with my emptiness. I started to realize that I moved to another city to run from my original hurt but there was no escaping it. I needed to deal with it. I stayed in Charlotte a few more months before everything there just fell apart. I lost my job, my sister lost her job, and we couldn't afford to stay any longer. We moved back to Greensboro at the beginning of the summer. In the back of my mind, I knew

I needed to go back to my first love – the Lord.

For a year, I floated from church service to church service with two of my sisters. We all needed to reconnect but more than anything, I felt really lost. One Sunday while sitting in a revival-like service, how to reconnect became plain. The man preaching reminded us so much of our father. We were all in awe of the message the preacher was preaching. All three of us felt like we were watching our father preach. His demeanor was so powerful and his message empowering. He wanted everyone in attendance to know that we were all loved by God and that there is *always* a way back to the Father.

As he prayed for each section in the church, you could see God moving. Once he got to our section it was as if a wave of mighty wind knock everyone down or back in our section. As the power of God moved, I felt a soothing calm hovering over me as if communicating, *"I love you and everything will be ok from now on."* I immediately lost it in a fit of praise! God still loved me and had forgiven me for EVERYTHING I had done. This was the start of my journey back to Christ.

As I began to reconnect with God, He reminded me daily through His Word that He loved me and that I belonged to him. My life was changing for the better and I was being directed to stay in his will. No, I haven't done everything right since, however God's grace and mercy towards me has kept me from leaving His side. He chose me so I've chosen him right back. I love the Lord and even though, at times, my walk can get hard, I'd rather have those difficult days knowing that because I'm chosen, He will always keep me safe. *"But you are not like that, for you are a chosen people. You are royal priests,[a] a holy nation, God's very own possession. As a result, you can show others the goodness of God, for he called you out of the darkness into his wonderful light"* (1 Peter 2:9, NLT).

ABOUT HARRIET

Harriet Grimes was born the seventh of nine children to Bishop Edward and Mamie Grimes in Saint Louis, MO. In 1990, her mother moved the family to Littleton, NC where she spent the majority of her childhood. Harriet was reared in an apostolic holiness church where her morals and values were shaped. She accepted Christ into her life at the age of nine and thus began her incredible journey with the Lord.

After the passing of her mother in 1999, Harriet moved to Greensboro, NC with three of her siblings. Once in Greensboro, she attended and graduated from Smith High School. Harriet attended the University of North Carolina - Greensboro for three years but did not complete the degree after realizing her passion was not there. Diligently searching for purpose, she worked in Customer service for six years before realizing her true passion was doing hair.

Harriet attended Leon's Beauty School and received her

certification for Cosmetology in 2013. She has spent the last five years as a Hairstylist, a friend, and a counselor to the many who sit in her chair. Throughout this journey, she has realized her true place in Christ and embraced that she has been chosen to lead in His kingdom.

Connect with Harriet at www.facebook.com/harriet.l.grimes

I Sing Because I'm Happy

Sheryl J. Yelverton

Wednesday, November 26, 2014 at 11:04 a.m. I woke up to a knock on my bedroom door. It was my husband telling me he needed to talk. However, what came out of his mouth, I was, in no way, prepared for. *"I'm giving you a heads up. This arrangement is not working for me and I need you out. You can take the vehicle that you are driving now* [which was his] *until you get one, so that you don't have to worry about getting to work."* You see, during this time I was working a night shift. I reported to work at 4:00 p.m. and didn't get off until 12:30 a.m. This often resulted in my not getting home until sometimes between 1:00 - 2:00 a.m. Still half asleep, I sat up so I could make sure I was hearing clearly. This was not my first time hearing these words, though, so when I sat up in the bed, I sat up so I could hear, but I also sat up to be able to protect myself in the event he wanted to reinforce his statement with a fist to my face. However, as I sat up, I realized I wasn't in shock. I knew this was coming!

Five months prior, we took a trip to support our two daughters at an event. While riding down the highway talking about several different subjects, I noticed the atmosphere changed as we began to speak of some life expectations. I listened quietly as I always did and said nothing. Which takes me back to why I sat up in bed and expected to be physically assaulted. Can you say "trigger mechanism?" (a physiological or psychological process caused by a stimulus and resulting in a usually severe reaction) I spent all three of our marriages together walking on egg shells trying not to trigger or push any buttons. (Yes, I said all three!) I have to own the fact that despite this, I knew how to push his buttons. (You do know we, women, know how to push buttons?)

Three months later the warfare intensified. *"For we wrestle not against flesh and blood, but against principalities, against powers, against the rulers of the darkness of this world, against spiritual wickedness in high places" (Ephesians 6:12, KJV).* The attacks came so severely at night, I felt I was in a constant fight to stay alive. The enemy would try and choke me in my sleep and wear me out. Every morning I woke up exhausted from the warfare. During this time, we had gone back to sleeping in two separate rooms. He would walk in the house and stonewall me like I was not even there. No communication whatsoever; not even a hello or how are you doing today? I would speak, however, I would not get a response. If there were words, they were words berating me, calling me names, and, tearing me down – again, trying to take life from me. Verbal and mental abuse was much worse than any physical abuse I could have ever endured or imagined. I feared for my life.

Certain behaviors did not go unnoticed. There were familiar patterns that he did not recognize. He had many generational seeds that were deeply rooted in his life and had grown deeper as the years went by. Unresolved childhood issues, strongholds of jealousy, bitterness, anger, rage, cruelty, and the deep pains that were never dealt with were showing their ugly heads again. His refusal to forgive and release the past had caused a demonic presence to become more powerful in him. The demonic influence and control in his life was so strong I could smell it. Yes, I could smell it. The old church mothers would say, *"I smell sin."* He had become a predator to me. The plan of the enemy from the beginning was to rob and deface (to mar the surface or appearance of, to disfigure) me of my giftings and anointing if not manipulation, by open force.

The fear and dread of going home was so over-whelming. It was not a healthy environment in which to live. My physical body was tired of dealing with the mental anguish. It was beginning to take its toll on me. The day the words *"I need you out"* came out of his mouth, I was so devastated. My heart was bleeding and broken because, despite his cruelty, I loved my husband. I took my vows and my covenant very serious – till death do you part. It is possible that you can experience death and still be alive. If you want to know what it feels like to go through separation and divorce, it feels like death.

That week the flood of emotions began to overtake me. I had to fight to keep my sanity. I almost lost my mind. The spirit of depression and discouragement tried to overtake me but I was determined to live and not die! I felt angry, hurt, and shamed again. The after effects of a broken relationship open the door for the enemy to drive a knife through your heart and reopen old wounds. My faith, hope, trust in God, and the very core of who I was was being challenged. Some days I didn't know what I was doing or if I was coming or going. I went to work, did my job, and went home. I prayed and cried out to God to take the pain away. This pain was familiar, however, this time, it was greater than any pain I'd ever experienced. I began to soul search and do self-examination. What was it in me that would continue to draw him to me and me to him? I married this man three times and it just didn't work. I trusted him to take care of me, but as in times past, it ended up that Jesus was taking care of me. He was true to

His Word, *"I'll never leave you nor forsake you" (Hebrew 13:5, KJV)*.

I had to reach back and stand on the foundational truths I was raised on. However, I must be transparent because some days I didn't want to do anything but get from point A to point B. That was all I could do. When I was growing up, my father could tell when I was going through something and he would make me sing. He would say to me, *"Sheryl, sing your way out,"* and I always did. I would sing until breakthrough and deliverance took place in my own life. To this day I still sing my way through. *"But I will sing of thy power; yea, I will sing aloud of thy mercy in the morning: for thou hast been my defense and refuge in the day of trouble" (Psalm 59:16, KJV)*.

I found out about a program on my job for employees to seek help for any life changing situations (EAP). I decided to seek help. I found a Christian Counselor and began counseling sessions. You must understand that for me to go to a therapist was a big deal because of how I was raised. Back then, seeing a therapist meant you were crazy and it was also considered a sin. Today I'm saying, to not seek counsel would be detrimental to your well-being. The healing process had begun.

Remember I said I wasn't in shock at his statement? The Friday before I received this devastating news, the Holy Spirit had me looking for a place to move. I was off that Friday, so I got up early that morning and began the search. I looked for places close to my job because this would make it somewhat easier for me to get back and forth in case of bad weather. The very first place I walked into had a vacancy. I completed the paper work and the second leasing agent walked me across the street to show me the available apartment. Upon returning to the leasing office, the agent that took my paperwork informed me that everything checked out and asked when I could move in. Can you say favor! The Lord had provided a way of escape for me! I cried and praised God all the way back to the house.

Once I returned home, I called my eldest daughter and told her what was going on and that I had secured a place to live. She instructed me to not move or touch any items in the house, but to go down to the storage area where I had the rest of my items stored and prepare those items to be moved so as not to arouse any suspicion. I did exactly as she had instructed me to do. I didn't have anything but clothes and a few kitchen items. Before we married, I sold or gave much of my household items away. She told me that she and my son-in-love would pack up everything inside the house when they arrived.

Moving day, I was awake early and up as soon as I heard my husband leave the house. The movers were scheduled to arrive at 8:00 a.m. They were delayed arriving, but I was up and preparing last minute items. As soon as my children arrived, we immediately began packing and moving my items to the truck. While packing, my daughter and I were immersed in conversation and we heard the door open. I thought it was one of the movers coming in to retrieve more items, so I didn't stop talking. However, my daughter could see from where she was standing that my husband had come in. For three months, he had stopped coming back to the house during the day. Wednesdays especially, he would stay away most of all of the day into the late night. But that day he decided to come back. Immediately, I was afraid. What am I going to do? I asked myself and then I asked my daughter. She immediately tells me, *"You're going to continue doing exactly what you're doing."* In that few seconds, he makes eye contact with her but says nothing. He grabs something off of his keyboard, turns around, and leaves. My daughter texted her husband, who was down the hill at the storage unit, to alert him of the situation. Before my husband could pull off, my son was at the top of the hill to make sure me and my daughter were ok. My husband left without incident and we continued to pack. I thank God I had double protection that day; my son and The Son!

In less than two hours, I was packed, moved, and sitting in a restaurant eating lunch with my daughters and son, recapping all that had just taken place. Later that evening, a peace came over me that I hadn't felt in a very long time. Don't get me wrong, the pain was still there, and the sting was there, but now, I had some sense of peace and I could rest. *"Thou wilt keep him in perfect peace, whose mind is stayed on thee: because he trusteth in thee" (Isaiah 26:3, KJV).*

In the weeks following, I took advantage of therapy that was offered to me. I didn't realize that was the best thing I could have done. I felt like I let family down. I knew I had to face them to answer questions that I wasn't ready to answer. More importantly, I felt like I let God down even though I knew He was with me. It was time for me to pick myself up though, dust myself off, and keep moving. I was determined to not give up. I continued my routine of getting up early to work and back home. I joined the gym and started working out. This was good for my physical and emotional health. I still cried and prayed many nights to God to take the pain away. Worshipping and meditating on God's Word brought me through. I placed yellow stickers with scriptures on the bathroom mirrors to keep the Word present before me, flowing in me, and through me. If I wasn't worshipping and making melody to God with my voice, I played worship music and worshipped.

God sent ministering angels to me on my job. People I didn't know came to minister to me. They would walk in, look at me, and immediately say, *"I don't know what you're going through, but God would have me give you this word."* Many times, I found myself in the back room at work because the presence of the Lord would over shadow me so. Everything about my life comes from my relationship with God. *"He that dwelleth in the secret place of the most High shall abide under the shadow of the almighty. I will say of the Lord HE IS MY REFUGE AND MY FORTRESS: MY God in Him will I trust" (Psalm 91:1-2, KJV).*

The transforming power of God gave me inner strength I never knew I had. Going through the process allowed me to be healed and not be destroyed or destroy myself. Please understand there had to be a soul searching and a willingness to be healed. I had to ask God to search me and if He found any wicked way in me, take it out and strengthen me. I repented of my sins and asked Him to show me areas of my life that did not please Him. I asked him to uproot any generational sins and curses that I may not have been aware of, and uproot and dig out any and all un-godly ties, negative thoughts and expectations. I pulled down every stronghold that sought to exalt itself against the knowledge of the will of God for my life. I fixed my eyes on Jesus and pressed forward in Him. *"Brethren, I count not myself to have apprehended: but this one thing I do, forgetting those things which are behind, and reaching forth unto those things which are before, I press [strain] toward the mark for the prize of the high calling of God in Christ Jesus" (Philippians 3:13-14, KJV).*

I literally woke up one morning with a healed heart and pain gone knowing that I had experienced the healing power of God.

I was no longer a battered woman, I was healed, set free, and delivered. Today, I have my voice back ready to declare and decree that the healing power of God is available to all. The old Sheryl is gone and I, now, walk in freedom. I don't have to doubt how far I can go. With everything I've faced, I know how far I have come, all the battles God has helped me win, and all the fears I've overcome. *"Therefore if any man be in Christ, he is a new creature: old things are passed away: behold, all things are become new" (2 Corinthians 5:17, KJV).* The saying holds true for me, *"I don't look like what I've been through."* However, I, now, sing because I am happy. I sing because I'm free. His eyes is on the sparrow and I know He watches me. I am a C.H.U.R.C.H. Girl through and through. I am Chosen, Holy, Unique, Resilient, Classy, and Healed to the glory of God. Amen!

ABOUT SHERYL

Sheryl accepted the Lord Jesus Christ as her personal savior at an early age, as well as being developed into her God given gift of singing and preaching.

Sheryl's initial ordination was through and by her father, the Late Bishop F. Yelverton of the Mount Calvary Holy Churches of America, Inc. She worked faithfully in ministry in the Durham church until she relocated to Charlotte, North Carolina in 1992.

Upon her arrival to Charlotte, she united with then the Salem Baptist Church, where Rev. Anthony L. Jinwright was Senior Pastor. She served as an Associate Minister and served on the board of College of Ministers and was reaffirmed as an ordained Elder in the Lord's Church As ministry in the church grew she implemented and introduced to this body of believers the Ministry of Worship and Praise. With such a passion and heart for the things of God, her ministry was birthed, Zion Ministries, Inc. Her charge from this ministry is to reach lost souls for the

Kingdom and encourage the body of Christ to worship the father in spirit and in truth.

Elder Yelverton currently attends Monument of Praise Ministries, Inc. under the leadership of Dr. Kevin A. Williams, High Point, North Carolina.

God has blessed Elder Yelverton with two beautiful daughters: Evangelist Tequita Brice, the visionary of the C.H.U.R.C.H. Girls Book Project and Psalmist Marlena Joyce Obie.

Connect with Sheryl at www.facebook.com/sheryl.yelverton

I Once Was Blind, But Now I See

Sandra McCullough

My story starts pretty simple. I grew in a two parent home and attended a private Christian school until 4th grade. Growing up, my parents always kept me in church. I was an usher, sang in the choir, attended Sunday School, and went to every revival. However, I quickly realized that though I spent time at church, the Word was not in me.

When I was about ten years old, my parents separated and we had to move to the projects. For a time, I remained in private school but, every day, I saw the kids that lived in our tenement getting on and off the school bus. I felt like I was missing out on something so I begged my mother to let my brother and I go to the school all the other kids attended. Even though my mom and dad no longer lived together, I still saw my dad every day. I was definitely a daddy's girl. My brother and I had different fathers but my dad treated my brother like he was his own.

My parents encouraged me to go to college after graduation but, at the time, I thought I was grown enough to make my own decisions. I had my own car my father purchased for me when I was in the 10th grade. I already had a full time job and thought I was living the life. I was a spoiled child. I didn't pay my car insurance or my car payment. As a matter of fact, I didn't have to pay any bills and I thought I was grown. Because everything was given to me, I really didn't learn how to be responsible. I didn't realize it then, but there were a lot of things I didn't learn at home. Even though, I saw my father every day, our relationship didn't equip me to be the best at making wise choices in relationships.

One Saturday while I was outside washing my car, a truck pulled up beside me. The guy on the passenger side asked for my number and without thought, I gave it to him. He called me later on that night and the rest, you could say, is history. I started driving to see him almost every day. He lived with his Aunt on the other side of town. During one of my visits, I found out from his Aunt that he was ten years my senior. She shared this with me while I sat with her waiting for her him to return. He often left me sitting there with her while he visited a house about three houses up from his aunt's house. I always wondered why he didn't take me with him. I felt like he didn't want his friends to meet me. Usually before he left to go there, he would ask to borrow money that he never paid back. He never took me to dinner or to do anything exciting. The only thing he wanted to do was get a motel room that I had to pay for. After a while, I started feeling used. This dude didn't work, didn't have a car, and didn't have any money but I kept seeing him because he had that talk that I fell for. When he finally introduced me to some of his friends, they told me the house up the street was a drug house and that I was basically financing his drug habit seeing as he would go use every time I went to see him. I also discovered he had a child and he was still messing around with the baby's mother. In true ghetto style, she came over to his house one afternoon I was there to meet me. She, of course, felt like she needed to share some information. The day he met me, he also met and had been seeing another girl who lived just five apartments down from me. That was enough for me.

I moved on to what I thought was bigger and better things. I was introduced to the club life and from Thursday to Sunday every week, I was partying, drinking, and having the time of my life. There wasn't a guy I met that I didn't go home with. I was nineteen years old coming and going as I pleased. I stayed out all night most weekends and did basically everything opposite of what I had been taught. Most of my friends didn't have a car so I was always the driver, however, my car was a moving violation. I always had a crowd of people in it, I often allowed others to drive that were not covered my by insurance if anything were to happen, and worst of all, I did a lot of drinking and driving.

One night, I was partying and drinking with friends. We passed around Private Stock and punch someone spiked with Everclear. In typical Sandra fashion, (you know I always had to do everything big) I asked for the bottle of Everclear without the punch and I drank it straight. If you know anything about this substance, it boasts to be 180 proof of straight alcohol. I drank so much, I passed out. Later that night, I thought I felt well enough to drive myself home. I was about a thirty minute drive away from home. I remember driving down the street to get to the highway. No sooner than I turned onto the highway, out of nowhere, I saw two white horses pass by in front of me. I must have blacked out because I didn't remember anything else when I came to the next day, not even how I made it home. All I knew was that I could have been destroyed that night. I could have suffered a car accident that ended my life but God's hand of protection was operating for me even though I wasn't living how I should have been living. From that moment to this one, I read Psalm 91, the prayer of protection and thank God for saving my life.

I truly believe that night was a wakeup call for me. Sadly, though, I did not heed it. It took no time for me to get back out there and continue partying and clubbing. I had a tendency to attract men who were more than ten years older than me. It wasn't until later in my life, I discovered that even though my father gave me things, he didn't provide enough emotional support to not leave me open and vulnerable to being taken advantage of by men who were predators.

Partying late one night, I met another man everyone called Big Daddy. His reputation of a ladies man preceded him and every woman I knew wanted a chance to be with him. When he paid me attention, I was all too thrilled. I was going to get a chance to see what the hype was all about. Unfortunately, I found out very quickly that that's all it was – hype. Like my previous relationship, he was on drugs. He also didn't have a job, or money, and had multiple female relationships. I allowed myself to keep sliding further and further into the abyss of the dysfunctional relationship. I found myself sneaking out of people's houses after having been with him because another female would show up. However, he was like a drug and I couldn't stop seeing him.

There were so many unfulfilled promises. He promised to take me to the beach one weekend. I was so happy to finally be doing something different and something that, in my mind, solidified that I was important and worthy. Sadly, we only ended up at the closest motel that, again, I had to pay for. I footed the bill for the room, the drugs, and the alcohol. While he was getting high, I was getting drunk. I was determined not to get hooked on drugs but he talked me into trying it. It wasn't a habit for me yet but the environment was so volatile, I don't know how I survived.

During our rendezvous no beach weekend, he ran out of drugs. He asked me go buy him more but I refused. He didn't like my response so he beat me black and blue. I didn't know what to do. I'd never been treated like this before. My spirit was broken but with my black eye and bruised lip, I ended up buying the drugs anyway. That night, though, I not only bought them, I used them. I began using crack cocaine on the weekends with him but it wasn't before long I started buying for myself. That night and every time I was with him after that night, I bought the drugs. I figured if I was buying them, I may as well smoke them too. I had become addicted. What started as an only on the weekend thing became an everyday thing. The very environment my parents tried to shield me from, I sought out. I embraced it. The toxic environment had become the place I felt most at home.

I started using my body to get the drugs I wanted. While my

dad was at work, I stole whatever money he had laying around, his guns, and his television and ran straight to the pawn shop to get money to buy drugs. When he got home from work and realized what I'd done, he would go buy back his things from the pawn shop and I would do it all over again the next day. Many times, he threatened to have me thrown in jail but he never did. I would get my paycheck and within an hour my money would be gone having paid no bills or purchased any food for the house. My Dad was always there picking up the slack. He paid his bills and mine. He put food in house and mine. I took my Dad through the most and his love for me never changed.

I got into yet another dead end relationship with someone who turned out to be a reminder that I reaped what I sowed. I was in a relationship with this man for seven years. We lived in an apartment together that my father put in his name for me. My life with him was the same: partying, drinking, and drugs, just more demeaning than all the others. When I ran out of money for my drugs, he would only give me drugs in exchange for what amounted to prostitution. He treated me horribly and I allowed it.

He received a settlement from an accident he'd been in after which he got missing for months. I didn't know if he were dead or alive so I moved on but three months later, he came back. I was in my apartment with the man I ended up marrying and this man knocked at the door. When I didn't open it, he tried to kick it down. I feared for my life so I ran. The next day I returned to my apartment to find that everything I had, from furniture to clothes, was gone. I had nothing left but the clothes on my back.

I had to go back to live with my mom. She did her best to try to help me in my addicted state but the pull was too strong. Nights when she went to sleep, I had the drug dealers come to my bedroom window to sell me drugs. I cannot tell you how many times I snuck out of the house through my bed room window. It would be two or three o'clock in the morning and she would hear me leave out. She would get up, get in her car, and ride down the streets trying to find me. I hid in bushes and behind other people's houses in an attempt to not be caught by her. She tried her best to protect me, at that moment, not just from drugs but from myself and I didn't make it easy for her. I'm thankful she loved me enough to keep fighting for me.

Everything I'd been through left me with a lot of insecurities. I constantly felt like I was fat, ugly, and not good enough. I was concerned about what others thought of me. I had been mistreated, used up, and betrayed all because I was looking for love in all the wrong places and doing all the wrong things just to fit in. I did my best to show love in all of my relationships but I was not shown love back. I was mostly treated like I didn't exist or that the only thing I had of value was what I had been given to make life. I had done so many things I was ashamed of but the Word of the Lord came to pull me out of the bondage I was so deeply caught in. *"There is therefore now no condemnation to them which are in Christ Jesus, who walk not after the flesh, but after the Spirit"* (Romans 8:1, KJV).

In March of 1996, I became pregnant with my only child. I used drugs at least eight of the nine months I was pregnant. I felt so convicted every time I used. I constantly prayed and asked God to protect my baby because he didn't have anything to do with my drug use. I wanted to stop so badly that I called the police on myself and asked to be picked up and put in jail. I figured if I was locked up, at least I couldn't use. The police told my mom if I had sense enough to call them, I had sense enough to stop using. I couldn't believe they didn't know it wasn't that simple.

December 20, 1996, my son was born via caesarean. I was so happy and relieved to have had no complications getting him into the world. My son was born healthy and handsome to the glory of God! After they cleaned him off and let me see him briefly, they whisked him away. It seemed my blood work revealed that I had used illicit substances and social services was alerted. They threatened to take my child. I was in turmoil! There was no way God would let my child be born healthy for me not to get to raise him. Thankfully, my mother intervened! She vouched that I lived with her and that she would be responsible for making sure I took care of my child.

Seven months later, July 12, 1997 to be exact, I was delivered from drug addiction. My struggle was over. I am thankful God protected me even in the foolishness I did to myself and to others. My life is a testament to the healing, saving, and delivering power of God! Not only did He free me from addiction, but from low self-esteem, and feeling like I less than nothing. I embraced 2 Corinthians 5:17 (NLT) *"This means that anyone who belongs to Christ has become a new person. The old life is gone; a new life has begun!"* Today, I am proud to be a C.H.U.R.C.H. Girl. God is still working on me, however, I don't look like what I've been through. He's perfecting me until He returns and that's a work that I welcome daily!

ABOUT SANDRA

Sandra P. McCullough was born and raised in High Point, North Carolina. She describes herself as a C.H.U.R.C.H. Girl who is still here by the grace of God.

Although Sandra was raised in the ways of God, she strayed away. As a result, her detour almost cost her life. She was delivered from a crack cocaine addiction on July 12, 1997. Since that time, God has favored her life.

Sandra works in sales where she gets to exercise her God-given gift connecting with people. From all the heartache, betrayal, and mistreatment that has happened in her life, she gives God all the praise for allowing her to be alive and to be a witness of His loving, saving grace. Sandra says she is on a mission to accomplish everything God has for her, walking by faith not by sight.

Sandra is a member of Monument of Praise Ministries where Dr. Kevin A. Williams is her pastor. She is family oriented, happily married to Jeffray McCullough, and is the proud mother of one son, Jeffray McCullough, Jr.

Connect with Sandra at www.facebook.com/sandra.mccullough.7.

Resilience Is My Portion

Kendra Diggs

He had brown skin, a wavy haircut, full eyebrows, and acute smile with a gap between his teeth. I noticed this man observing me every time I led Praise and Worship and every time I walked around to put my offering in the collection plate. I loved when I saw him come into church with his Express button up shirts. He was just, in the words of OutKast, *"so fresh and so clean."* He came in and sit in the exact same spot every Sunday and Wednesday. When we finally bumped into each other, a smile came across his face as he introduced himself. I shook his hand and smiled as well. I looked in his eyes and I knew instantly he was interested in me, but I didn't want to assume. I had had my share of unsuccessful relationships that I didn't care to repeat, so I just stayed to myself for a while.

We found each other on Facebook because I became Sherlock Holmes and I did some serious research on who he was. From what I saw, he seemed pretty cool. We exchanged numbers through Facebook Messenger. The next morning he consistently texted me throughout the day. I was very impressed, but I didn't want to get too involved as of yet. However, we quickly graduated from text messages to hanging out more. I didn't have a car so he would pick me up for Bible Study and we hung out at the bookstore from time to time. We had very similar tastes as far as growing up in the 90s with our favorite cartoons like X Men, Power Rangers, Rugrats, and in music and food. We talked on the phone for hours. We fall asleep and woke each other up. We prayed together. He listened to me and made me feel like he really heard what I had to say. He was different just like me and I felt myself opening up to him more and more. He became my best friend and over time, we began to date.

He knew all of my weaknesses but yet it seemed he accepted me for me. My flaws, my imperfections, and my quirkiness he loved and likewise, I embraced him for who he was. He had a really dark past, but I thought in my mind, "*I shouldn't pass him up because of that, he would never do those things to me….or would he?*" Christmas Day he proposed to me in front of my family. We had talked about marriage a few months before and I told him with tears in my eyes, "*I don't want to ruin your life, I don't think I'm ready.*"

He grabbed my hand and looked at me intently, *"We will get through this together. I need you."* He kissed me on my lips gently and I felt reassured.

I was still very dependent. I lived at home with my parents. I didn't know how to be on my own and I was still a virgin. I didn't have any experience with anything, but that didn't stop him from marrying me. He reassured me all would be fine and we would work on things together. Our wedding day was amazing. All of our friends and family came to celebrate with us but the downfall was, I was on my monthly cycle which crushed me. The birth control I was taking landed right on the day of my wedding that my cycle would start.

A few days after we married, I made love for the first time. I was terrified but he was very patient with me. I had never felt that way before. I felt like I could be in his arms forever. I felt like I finally belonged. It was the best feeling of being with someone who truly valued you, loved you, and was willing to wait until marriage to be intimate with you. I thought this would be my happily ever after, however, things began to change a couple of months later. Tension arose, arguments infused, and when I began to gain weight, he no longer found me attractive. He told me to my face that I was, "stiff," and that my body was not proportionate. I was heavier when we were dating but I slimmed all the way down for our wedding day. I really didn't understand the issue.

He told me I was slowing him down if I went to the gym with him or even when I end up going to the gym with him, he left me by myself. If we ran together, he would outrun me and never wait. And from time to time, I was physically abused. He had a lot of anger issues and he didn't know how to keep his hands to himself but I loved him and I stayed. One day I found something that I never thought I would find. I went on his computer, searched his history, and found nothing but porn sites. I was devastated. I confronted him about it with tears in my eyes. *"What is it that these women do that I can't do?"* I screamed with tears rolling down my face. With no remorse on his face, my husband said, *"I'm sorry Kendra."* I turned to him with my eyes burning from the tears, *"Don't you love me? Why are you doing this to me?"* He sighed and said, *"Kendra, they don't mean anything to me. I won't look at it again."* My heart was racing, I felt betrayed.

I did everything that he wanted. Even things I was uncomfortable doing sexually. Why was I not enough? Since everyone knew what was going on in our personal lives, months later we decided to move to another city. We had done enough damage in my our home town so he thought we might as well start over. I was not agreeable with this decision at all, however I went along with it. I was still dealing with my weight issue and the subject of porn with my husband. It was an empty promise. He still watched it and I began to become desperate. *"What can I do to make him happy and in love with me again?"* I thought to myself sorrowfully. Desperate to find a solution to my problem, I made the decision to be open to watching it.

What does a church girl know about pornography? Nothing. I heard how it could affect the mind and how it could damage your perspective on sex, but to make my husband happy I told him I was open. Plus, I thought I could possibly learn a thing or two right? We set a day for us to watch it together. I lay beside him in our bed and he went to a website. As soon as the images appeared on the screen, a rush came over me. My heart began to beat fast. My body was on fire. My husband began to kiss my neck softly and asked if I was okay. As he began to take off my clothes, I couldn't take my eyes off the screen. A release came over me. It felt so good, but quickly I started to feel guilty. I wanted my husband happy and maybe just maybe if I keep watching these videos, I reasoned within myself, I can make my husband fall in love with me again. Chaos began to consume us.

Everywhere we went, drama followed us. I became more stressed and I ended up turning to porn to help me with it. I loved the feeling and rush I got from it. The sensation made me feel great. I was addicted and didn't even realize it. Our marriage became toxic and dysfunctional and it was coming closer and closer to a close. He changed the passwords to his phone and his e-mails so I wouldn't have any access to what he did. After he worked he would take a shower, leave for hours, and wouldn't come back home until the next morning reeking of alcohol and weed. One night I also turned to drinking to numb my pain and all I could do was cry. I knew my marriage was over.

One weekend, I went back home to visit my family and to celebrate my niece's birthday. When I returned, I came home to find out I was kicked out the house and my husband didn't want to have anything else to do with me. I was crushed! I know I wasn't perfect and I made my mistakes in our marriage, but kicking me out knowing I didn't have anywhere else to go and that I still had my job in the city I felt was uncalled for. I ended up moving in with a friend of mine and stayed with her for a few months. However, to deal with my stress, loneliness, and the void I felt, I turned to porn again. It even got to the point where I would moan my husband's name. I was going down in a whirlwind of despair. I couldn't survive on my own and I went from bad to worse.

I started to take pills to numb the pain. I was so hurt and unhappy. My friends begged me to come back home. I didn't want to because of my job. I didn't want to be around anyone, but I didn't have any other choice. Either I would go back to my toxic husband, which I knew would eventually be deadly if I went back, or go back home with family. I conceded. I went back home. I was bitter and embarrassed. I had to go back home to face the people who didn't even want our marriage to exist. I was still addicted to porn and taking pills to numb the pain. I was devastated. I was depressed. I wanted to die and take my life. I went home and I took my pills again, I lay down on my bed and a rage burned inside of my chest. Tears began to roll down my face. I yelled. I screamed. I grabbed my head and cried, *"I'm tired, please just let me die."* I cried myself asleep. I didn't know how I was going to get out of the dark place I was in.

Then, on April 15, 2016, I had an encounter with God. I went on a retreat just to get away with God. It was the best thing I could have ever done. To realize that a holy Deity and someone so perfect loved and was in love with someone so imperfect like me, was just perfect. His unfailing love. It made me believe I could conquer anything. The things I turned to couldn't fill that void because only God could fill it. God became my covenant partner again, the shield around my heart. I had never felt more happy and at peace. I experienced peace beyond my understanding.

Of course, after I got my freedom, everything came at me. I had to fight even harder after my divorce was finalized to remain celibate. I was used to sex and porn. Every now and again I would slip back into it. I would choose myself and my flesh over God's voice saying no. Then I noticed that all of these guys were into me, but they only wanted one thing from me — sex. I lost a lot of weight and I guess a lot of different men saw that so my inbox was blowing up all of the time. I had to learn the difference between being valued and wanted. I had to learn and am still learning how to be by myself, enjoy my own company, and love me. One of the reasons people turn to sex and porn is because they desire intimacy, they desire to be *one* with someone.

I had to realize that intimacy, the real intimacy that I desired, only God could fill. God loves us so much and He wants us to know Him in an intimate way. He wants us to be holy as He is holy. That is what He desires. Everything I went through was necessary. It made me the woman I am and am still becoming today. I'm not perfect. I still struggle with insecurities and a lot of different emotions from time to time, but I am grateful for my story. I am grateful that He placed in me the ability to bounce back from every situation I could possibly go through. I realize every day that I am stronger than what I think and that God chose me for this time. I am one of His masterpieces in the earth. I am fearfully and wonderfully made and marvelous is His work in me — this my soul knows passionately!

ABOUT KENDRA

Kendra Diggs seemed to be born for a career in beauty. From a very young age, she was interested in makeup. She would watch her mother apply her make-up for church and studied her intently. Although she would dabble and do her own makeup, it wasn't until her high school matriculation that she began to practice her craft on others, honing her skills as an artist by lending her talents to the schools' Drama Department for plays and musicals. In 2010, her career jump started when she accepted a position with Bovanti. She was able to grow even more in her craft and realized she truly has a passion to help uplift women with her gifts.

Kendra transitioned into a M.A.C. Artist position in 2014 and has truly flourished. She aspires to change the world of beauty and see makeup artistry not only as a career, but as her ministry and her calling. She, also, aspires to empower women through self-love and sees beauty as a powerful way to accomplish that goal. She is motivated by seeing the pure joy on women's faces when she hands them the mirror after she has finished their makeup; that positive energy can truly fill your spirit. She has been faced with and overcome many obstacles she should not have survived, but God.

Through her gifts, Kendra endeavors to help other women not succumb to adversity and see their potential as well. She has a genuine passion for helping women to feel beautiful and radiate from the inside out.

Connect with Kendra at www.facebook.com/mrskendrafostermua

REFLECTION OF REALITY

Lakesha Holiday

In 2012, Tasha Cobbs released the worship song, "Break Every Chain". While this was not an original song, the song undeniably gained an unprecedented level of popularity – especially with me. Up until this time, I had never personally heard of the song. It was during this same time, that I was coming into an interconnectedness, reconciling past decisions that had left me scarred, broken, and seemingly unrepairable with the healing I was experiencing. I was at a place where I truly felt the Lord's love lift me, as the hymnologist so eloquently penned it, and while my journey was unknown, I, somehow, knew that I would come out alright.

In March 2013, I attended a Worship Encounter hosted by Pastor Cassandra Elliott (who happens to be a contributing author in this book!) During this encounter, I truly surrendered all that I had left and all that I had been holding on to. I will never forget that brisk and chilly evening. The lights were dimmed and "Break Every Chain" was being led in the background by Pastor Elliott and her worship team. I was in kneeling position, praying, and crying out to God. As my eyes were closed, I, literally and ever so vividly, imagined myself in a landfill. The sky was painted hues of pinks and subtle oranges and cranes where whipping through the early evening winds. As "Break Every Chain" was being ministered ever so powerfully, I could audibly hear the chains that sustained the cranes in the sky falling to the ground. As these large, metal chains hit the earth, I knew it represented the chains that had me bound. I experienced immense joy in knowing that freedom was literally in my reach. While still kneeling, I opened my eyes and looked in front of me. Through the glare of the stage lights that were shining through the darkness onto the worship team, I saw him. He had gotten to the event late, and due to the late hour, and the lack of seats, he was standing behind the last row of seats where I had been kneeling. I never knew the significance of that moment until years later.

After the Worship Encounter was over, a friend and I went to grab a bite to eat. Unbeknownst to me, he had invited a friend to join us. When we pulled up to the restaurant, I realized that this friend was the same guy I had just seen at the Worship

Encounter standing in front of me. As the night went on, we were introduced, and shortly thereafter, connected with one another on social media. The rest, as they say, is history. For a long time, an unfathomable history that I never believed I would ever be able to pick up a pen to write about. My assignment in sharing my story is not to craft a tell all memoir, but to simply give an account of an encounter I had with the Savior who changed my life when I thought it couldn't be changed. However, I know that in order for you to appreciate the value in my transparency, I have to lay the foundation.

As in every "love story" that begins as such, you can imagine what happened after we connected on social media. We literally became inseparable. We talked on the phone frequently and hung out more and more. We, eventually, ended up living together. For all the judgmental folk, I am a church girl to the core. I grew up in church and came into my own conviction and relationship with Jesus as a result. Religion nor relationship was forced upon me. Growing up, I enjoyed maturing in Christ. I knew living with someone whom you were not married to was a big no-no. Nevertheless, I knowingly rebelled against what I knew to be right. Whatever my reasons, I told myself it was because I wanted to be a loyal help to someone I liked a whole lot, who appeared to me to be struggling with a financial hardship as we all have experienced at some, or multiple, times in our lives. During the early days of our relationship, there were numerous red flags I encountered that led me to believe my decision to date this guy was neither a healthy, nor wise decision to make. I didn't necessarily believe that he was a bad person, I just believed that he chose to make bad decisions that affected others greater than they affected him. He was a product of an unhealthy environment of bad decisions others made regarding him as a child. Nevertheless, I chose to ignore these red flags because I wanted to show him I could be "different". I wanted to be the one that did not give up on him. I wanted to be the one to graciously pardon him from offense after offense – just to show him that someone could love and care for him beyond his imperfections, even when it wounded me in the process.

I guess you could say that I am cut from a different cloth. You see, I have this thing about me that, for a long time, I did not understand. I have this uncanny ability of covering people that, from the outside looking in, don't deserve to be covered. Unlike most, I don't take pleasure in exposing others' proclivities even at my own expense. Call it a character flaw or whatever you may, it's just not my makeup. Without disclosing two years of encounters I had with this individual, I will say that a defining moment came for me one evening after we had gotten into a pretty heated argument. I honestly have forgotten what even prompted the disagreement. All I remember is that I simply had no more energy to continue going back and forth, so I decided to end my contribution to the discussion by going silent. This did not go over well with him. Within a matter of moments, I felt a gust of wind fly by my face as I watched the lamp crash into my closet door. To this day, I do not know how that lamp missed me, especially with it close enough to my face to have felt the wind. However, it was at that moment I realized I had to make some critical decisions concerning my safety and my well-being.

Physically, I had become unrecognizable. My weight soared, my smile disappeared, and it was nothing for me to cry at the sheer thought of the life that had become my reality. I can't tell you how many co-pays were rendered on my behalf to doctors for the sake of my declining health. Spiritually and emotionally, I felt like the walking dead. I loved this man with every fiber of my being. I just wanted him to do something I later realized he was not capable of – loving me back. And not just loving me for the sake of being in relationship with me, but loving me right and healthy.

Shortly after the lamp incident, I decided to end the relationship. I can't tell you how difficult it was to stick to that decision. There were several times I faltered and failed to stand my ground. I allowed him to guilt me into giving him another shot to redeem himself. While we were no longer living together,

I still entertained him enough to where I can admit, it did not appear that I was serious in my decision to end the relationship. Enough was enough. I don't recall the precise details of where I was that day or what was on my mind, but I can say that I had reached my breaking point. I was finally willing to tread through unknown and unfamiliar territory to the discovery of my future without him. I totally ignored his advances. I blocked him on social media and his phone number. Of course, he did not make it easy for me, but I knew a man who had made my process doable for me over two thousand years ago on the cross. You see, Jesus did not just die for the pardon of my sins, but His blood was shed, He died, He was buried, and He was resurrected for my ability to see even the most difficult decisions through. Because of His grace, I didn't die where I was nor the state I was in.

In the years following, I totally rediscovered Lakesha and I did not like who I had become. I went into a period of hibernation where I had to learn to love myself all over again. I did, however, make a conscious decision to surround myself with women of God who could pray for me, cry with me and for me, fast on my behalf, and simply listen to me vent. From this experience, one thing I believe is this – Isolation is not of God! God loves on us through people. We encounter God through people He chooses to use, often. So the moment you allow your situation to isolate you and shut you off from people around you who truly love and care about you, is the moment you prolong your process. There is a difference in God calling you to a season of solitude, versus the enemy leading you into a wilderness of isolation. You have to know the difference.

As I continued to rediscover who I was, I noticed that I slowly regained my smile. I totally revamped my eating habits and transitioned to a plant based lifestyle. I became consistently active in my church ministry again. You see, I had become so lost in that toxic and unhealthy relationship, I totally lost sight of doing what made me happy and using the gifts and abilities that God had given me to pursue my purpose. Once I was back on track, I began to flourish in my purpose of mentoring children, in particular, Generation Z which is ages eight to twenty-one. I launched several products, enhanced my business endeavors, changed careers into doing what I love, went back to school, and so much more! Now, I do not want you to think that I achieved any of this on my own. As Psalms 118:23 (NLT) says, *"This is the Lord's doing, and it is wonderful to see."* In fact, many of the above accomplishments, even the unmentionable ones, I attempted to do on my own and failed, sometimes more than once. I don't know if you can relate to my story at all. Maybe you find yourself at the crossroads of making a tough decision, like I did, to abandon what or who you love that is toxic and unhealthy, for the sake of living a life of undeniable joy, ferocious freedom, and an unshakable truth of your value and self-worth. Regardless of where you may be, one thing is for sure, the journey of choosing you is impossible without God. He is the air we breathe. He is the ability in which our limbs are able to move and the wherewithal in which we even have the activity of our senses. Acts 17:28 (KJV) reminds us that we are the offspring of God, and in Him, we live, and move, and have our being.

Remember in the beginning of this chapter, I told you that I didn't realize the significance of my first time seeing the individual that I saw reflected in the glare of the stage lights until years later. I remember initially thinking that seeing him in that moment, was a "sign" of my new life; my sign of giving love another chance, my sign of pouring into, and my sign of investing into someone who needed me, just as much as I needed him. I was so vested into making and crafting the moment to be about me and limiting it to my own perception, that I never cross referenced that encounter with God. Once I did, years later, God revealed to me that He wasn't showing me a reflection of what I could have, but a reflection of what I was to never return to again after having just experienced freedom in Him through Christ. Whether it be in terms of a relationship, a decision regarding a career change, or the potential of a life altering yes or no to a person, place, or thing, ALWAYS seek the Lord regarding your decision. Don't be so quick to rely on your own failing intelligence to be your guiding compass. Jeremiah 29:11-13 (NLT) says, *"For I know the plans I have for you, says the Lord. "They are plans for good and not for disaster, to give you a future and a hope. In those days when you pray, I will listen. If you look for me wholeheartedly, you will find me."* Had I sought the Lord *before* making my decision, I could have avoided that hurtful detour in life. But you know what? Romans 8:28 (NLT) reminds me of this blessed assurance I will forever have, *"And we know that God causes EVERYTHING to work together for the good of those who love God and are called according to his purpose for them!"* Everything! Even the mess we get ourselves into!

If I could leave you with one more thing, it would be a glimpse into what the practical side of my healing process looked like. People often offer spiritual insight, but fail to provide you with practical ways in which you can incorporate and apply resources and tools through your process. Journaling worked for me. It was extremely therapeutic. I sought a licensed professional counselor for mental health therapy. As it relates to my career and business aspirations, I invested in myself by attending conferences that were centered around and geared towards my professional endeavors and goals. I hired a branding coach to help me redefine the brand and message of my business. I networked with people in and outside of my field. I began paying off all debt including student loans and I shifted my focus to, literally, serve my community. Outside of my local church, I cooked and prepared homecooked meals for local shelters, assembled care packages, (most of the time with my own money even when I didn't have a lot of it) and so much more.

It is truly by the grace of God that I not only survived, but that I overcame what the enemy meant for evil. What's even more amazing, I still love that individual with the love of Christ. I pray for him, and I sincerely desire God's best for him even though God's best for him was not me. It is with that same grace, and by the same measure of God-inspired maturity, dignity and class, that I pray for you. You are loved by me…but most importantly, you are loved by God!

ABOUT LAKESHA

Lakesha comes from four generations of Pastors, Evangelists, Teachers, and Missionaries of the Christian faith. Needless to say, Proverbs 22:6 King James Version, "Train up a child in the way he should go: and when he is old, he will not depart from it," was the foundation of her upbringing. From the age of five, she spent years being actively involved in just about every facet of church ministry: Outreach ministry, Music ministry, Youth and young adult ministries, Planning committees, Cleaning and everything in between.

The purpose of her sharing her heart's song of healing and restoration is not to expose the victimizer, but to strategically position every reader to the love, healing, forgiveness, and restoration of a Savior, who according to Galatians 5:1, allows you to stand fast therefore in the liberty wherewith Christ hath made you free; *and whose saving grace* will keep you from being entangled again with the yoke of bondage.

Lakesha enjoys serving Generation Z as a youth mentor and transparent motivational speaker. She calls herself the Master Dream Unlocker in which she nurtures dreamers into lifelong achievers through personal and professional development. She is an Entrepreneur and works in Public Education as a Youth Development Coordinator for a Title 1 School.

Lakesha believes in strategic partnerships and collaborations, as well as, serving others within their respective vision.
Connect with Lakesha via her website www.lakeshaholiday.com or at info@lakeshaholiday.com.

Resilience through Relationship

Kareen Hartley

I was jarred awake by the throbbing pain in my lower back. The baby was bearing down more than ever on my womb now. I was startled but I knew full well the moment I had been dreading was drawing near. Slowly, I pulled myself off the bed and scrambled around the room in the dark, trying to find the nearest wall that could support me as I hobbled to the bathroom. For the last six months this had been my routine – being awakened in the night as a result of one discomfort or another. When it wasn't sharp pains darting up and down the left side of my body, it was nausea or the constant need to urinate. Sleep was now a rarity in my life. Exhaustion was my norm.

I sighed in deep regret because I hoped this experience would have been much different. My previous pregnancy was nothing like this one. I was active and energetic. I worked up until the eight month of my pregnancy doing play therapy with a beautiful, autistic child. I also enjoyed daily walks, prepared meals at home and did housework regularly. I was happy and waiting with hopeful expectancy to see our child.

However, this pregnancy was radically different. I experienced nausea for the entire duration of the pregnancy. The constant vomiting made it difficult to regulate my eating habits. I was either binge eating due to the extreme feeling of hunger or going without food for long periods because of the intense nausea. Since I was sick all the time, working was absolutely out of the question. Regular walking also became a thing of the past. Lethargy and fatigue became my constant companions. Mornings and nights were the hardest and it had become almost impossible for me to effectively homeschool my son.

We were in our first year of, officially, starting to homeschool. I had a full year of scheduling planned but was only able to engage in about a third of our program. Most of our learning exploits were done on my bed. We were relegated to incessant book reading engaging our imagination more than we normally would to compensate for the reduction in high-energy, hands on activities and projects.

My son was struggling. He wasn't used to seeing me like this and was constantly worried about when I would start to feel better and resume our normal lives again. Although I had the support of family and friends, navigating life was still incredibly difficult. My husband was working double shifts — at work and when he got home. He was helping out with cooking, cleaning, and even school trips with our son. He tried to be available when I needed to talk and was always ready to give spiritual encouragement when I needed it. My brother and grandmother who lived with us at the time, also assisted with schooling, entertainment, meal prep, and providing emotional and spiritual support for myself and my son. Despite all this help, I fought anxiety and depression daily during the first half of the pregnancy. I felt alone and misunderstood. No one was able to help me undo the erratic and disruptive discomforts that rifled through my mind and my body.

 I hated it. Desperate and consumed with doubts, I cried out to God. I felt angry and confused. With no answers, I started comparing the dynamics of my life during my first pregnancy. I wasn't married at the time and not really living according to the standards He wanted me to uphold. Yet, I had a normal and mostly uneventful experience. However, this pregnancy was within the confines of holy matrimony which I felt was orchestrated by Him. So, why was I suffering so much? He was pleased with me now, wasn't He? As a child of God who was living in alignment with the Holy Scriptures as best as I could, shouldn't my present life experiences look different from the times when I was not being obedient to His Word? Wasn't it God's responsibility to shield me and guard me from difficult circumstances like these? I felt unprotected and broken. I was angry and perturbed. What was God doing and when would He intervene? I knew He was there. I talked to Him every day about all of it. Some days, I felt like he had disappeared. Or, was it I who was no longer listening?

Most days, I tried to be grateful for the things that were going well but things got increasingly challenging. For example, around the six month of the pregnancy, I showed up at my doctor's office with the intent of doing a routine checkup, when my midwife observed that my last set of blood pressure readings were highly elevated. She inquired about the state of my hands and feet which were now frequently swollen. It was enough to bring on concern. She consulted with her nursing team and decided to request additional tests to rule out any impending abnormalities. At the mere mention of the words "additional tests," I sensed a slow and deliberate feeling of panic rise up within me. The flash of assaulting thoughts flooded my mind, *"You knew you were not strong enough physically to be carrying a baby. You knew your body was weak and ill prepared. You were not eating well. You were not thinking well. This was inevitable."*

As the thoughts came more quickly, the panic grew stronger. Through all the noise, I heard a firm but calm voice say, *"You are not only your body! You are also soul and spirit. My Spirit resides in you and your body is the temple of the Most High God. No one on else determines how capable you are through this process except Me and you. Trust Me. It doesn't matter what those numbers say. You are fine. Now, allow me to carry you through this journey."* I was elated and instantly soothed at the voice of the Lord silencing those negative thoughts. It had been such a long time since I'd heard His voice so clearly. Immediately, the feeling of panic was distilled and I completed every other test that was required with a sense of peace I hadn't experienced in a long time.

After I heard the voice of the Lord speak to me so clearly, I was hooked and promised myself never to go to another doctor's appointment without, first, committing my mind, body, and spirit to His wisdom and care. A few weeks later, as my midwife examined me, there was, again, concern that the baby hadn't turned according to the projected timeline. I was determined not to worry. As she continued to speak, I prayed and asked the Lord to intervene and remove any complications that were threatening to interfere with my own life or that of our baby. I firmly believed that every negative situation that presented itself would be fully resolved by God.

I was reminded of how the Lord had prompted me to start

spending more time with Him after my previous doctor's visit. He showed me how, over the years, I believed things about Him that were not true and how those lies produced chaos for me on a daily basis. He revealed that when my life was going smoothly, I wouldn't long to be with Him as much as I did when things were going wrong. I would cut myself off from His guidance and direction — limiting myself to my own perceptions and not benefiting from His 360 degree view of my life.

I immediately repented and I told him how sorry I was. From that time, I began to allow Him to direct our moments together. It was freeing and transformative. I was now on a path where what He said would be the guide for how I went about my days. With confidence that only God could provide, I announced to my doctor that I understood her concerns but was strongly convinced that both myself and my baby were fine. However, for the sake of her peace of mind, I would submit to the ultrasound and further observation.

I didn't leave the hospital as planned that day. I spent the entire day doing assessments. As I waited for results, I listened to Bible verses on my phone and chatted with all the nurses who were confused at how calm I was. I asked them about their own relationships with God and had a good time sharing how He was helping me to transition from being worried and anxious about the process to being calm and confident in Him. I also reached out to family and friends and asked them to pray.

After a number of hours, the head of gynecology declared that he was officially not worried and I was free to go home. He told me to gets lots of rest and stay off my feet. *"No more stressors,"* he said. I explained to him that when I was home I felt calm but every visit to the hospital resulted in some type of stressful episode. The endless tests the medical staff insisted on carrying out caused me much anxiety. The constant back and forth was enough to keep anyone stressed out. He understood but insisted that I complete stress-tests for the final weeks leading up to delivery, so we could keep a close eye on the baby. When He left the room, I worshipped and gave God thanks for His continuous reassurance. Acknowledging that in the midst of the constant bad news, He was always in charge.

After two consecutive weeks of stress assessments, the results were the same. The baby was doing fine. I was relieved and determined to spend the last two weeks before my delivery in prayer, as I sensed there was an impending storm ahead.

On delivery day, things moved rapidly. I was admitted and prepped for the occasion within mere hours before the baby's appearance. When the nurses examined me, I was almost fully dilated. I was, quickly, assigned to a nearby room as the nursing team put everything into place. It was my second time giving birth so the routine was familiar. The contractions were rapid and fierce as the nurses alerted me to started pushing. I yielded to their coaching with intense focus while I, silently, prayed for strength. My body felt battered from the onslaught of pain coursing through my body. As I lay on the bed writhing and wincing, I noticed with every command to push that my energy was quickly waning. I began to feel strangely weak and my efforts to push slowly diminished. Again, that gnawing and relentless fear roused its head. I shuddered at the thought of my baby not surviving this process if I couldn't find the energy to get this job done. I could see the look of concern on the faces of the doctors and nurses. Their eyes darted rapidly from me to all the devices set up to monitor our progress. My husband moved in closer and spoke words of encouragement in my ear.

"*I can't do it*" I, nervously, said to him. "*I am trying really hard to find the energy but I just can't do it!*" He held my hand tighter, in assurance. By now, a few more doctors entered the room. I could vaguely hear them conferring urgently with each other, determining their next step as they noted the steady climb of my blood pressure. Suddenly, one of the nurses who examined me came right over to my bedside. She leaned towards me with a wagging finger and firmly said, "*Look, I know you can do this! I want to you to take the biggest breath you can find and give me the hardest push you can muster. Do you hear me?*" It was as if God was speaking to me directly through her. I, immediately, shifted into position, bracing myself for God to do something supernatural. *"Neither myself nor my baby is going to die on this bed in this hospital room today,"* I whispered to myself as I attempted one last push. Moments later, the room erupted in cheerful celebration as my daughter's head appeared before their eyes. I was elated and overwhelmed with tears. God had come through for me again. In the midst of my fear and weakness, His strength carried me. I could feel God's presence in the room as He reminded me that there would never be a storm big enough to crush me because He is always with me.

About Kareen

Kareen K. Hartley never dreamt of being a mother or a wife. In fact, since high school, she was always set on becoming an influential entrepreneur and philanthropist.

Kareen is a giver. That passion first became a reality when she served as a leader for Youth for Christ in her home country of Jamaica. Later, as she served as a discipleship leader in her local church she developed a hunger to study the Scriptures more deeply. This led to two life changing years at Bible School where she learned the value of effective mentorships and spiritual coaching.

Subsequently, Kareen relocated to the U.S. where she nurtured her interest in serving others by pursuing a degree in Behavioral Science. Although she also had a background in Health-Care Management and Play Therapy, she now describes her greatest achievements as being a wife, mom, and home educator.

Kareen uses the wisdom gained from all her life experiences to fuel her goals of entrepreneurship - as an author and a life coach. She helps like-minded women to overcome extreme exhaustion and reconnect with their purpose and passions in a way that revitalizes and energizes them.

Kareen has also contributed to an anthology called *"The Evolution Project"* - a collection of fun and entertaining tales about Migration, Family, Perseverance, Success, and Personal Growth. She is currently writing her first devotional, *"Refreshed and Refocused: A Biblical Approach to Getting your Drive Back."*

You can learn more about Kareen at www.towardsloving.com.

BROKEN TO BE MADE WHOLE

Shauntia Stanback

Why did it take him pulling a gun out on me before I realized how toxic things were? This is a question I had often asked myself. I didn't want to address it because I was too embarrassed to admit the abuse I had been enduring for years. How could this be me? I'm way too intellectual. How did I get to this point? What would people say? These were all the thoughts and feelings that plagued me.

Why should it even matter to me? Behind the façade of seeming very confident, outgoing, and seemingly having it all together, I was broken. Full of fear, anxiety, and self-doubt. I had become good at wearing a mask. The public persona I strived to have, never matched up with the personal hell I lived in. I had pretended for so long that I didn't even know who I was anymore.

I was beginning to become physically ill because of all the dis-ease I had been going through.

I remember the night it all changed. We had just come home from a birthday gathering. The argument started on the ride home. It was the usual; I seemed to have entertained a conversation a little too long. You would think we weren't seated at the same table, next to each other. In his opinion, I was giving someone more attention than I was giving him. Here we go again I thought, but this time was different. I was tired mentally, emotionally and physically. *"I'm not doing this with you tonight."* I proceeded to go to the bathroom to undress and get myself ready for bed. He had been drinking too much and I didn't feel like dealing with his drama.

As I got up off the bed to go into the bathroom, he blocked my entrance. I made several attempts to go around him trying to keep an argument from ensuing. He was nitpicking and I knew it. I was determined I was not going to allow him to get a rise out of me. This pattern of dysfunctionality had become our norm. Sometimes I felt as if he intentionally started arguments so he could have a reason to storm out of the house and leave, but not tonight. I wanted him gone and I didn't have the energy for an argument. I said to him, *"Instead of creating an argument, just leave because that's really what you want to do anyway."* I guess it was the nonchalant tone in which I made the comment because it seemed to set something off in him. The argument began anyway.

That night, everything I had ever thought came out. I wanted him to hurt in the same way he had hurt me emotionally over the years. I made some very emasculating comments. At the moment, I felt justified in all that I said; and truthfully, it felt good. It was if a load had been lifted. No longer did I suppress my comments for the sake of not wanting an argument to linger on for longer than necessary. I had become too predictable. He knew my way of dealing with things was actually not to deal with them at all, but not this night. He wanted to go there, so I went there right with him. All of my thoughts and feelings regarding him, the marriage, and all the affairs came spewing out like a volcano that had just erupted.

Over the years, this man had me on an emotional roller coaster that left me feeling numb and hopeless. I stayed on way longer than I should have. Eventually I begin to realize that I possessed the power to get off this ride and no longer deal with the dizzying effect of being in a loveless marriage. It was crazy the things I allowed myself to endure all in the name of what I thought was love.

One of the most painful moments over the span of our years together was the loss of our daughter. I gave birth to my precious Kennedy prematurely as a result of so much traumatic stress. I went into labor when I was 5 ½ months pregnant. Sadly, she passed 47 minutes after being born; her lungs were significantly underdeveloped. The pain of her loss was so unbearable and I went into a state of depression for a long time, believing I caused my daughter's death because of the many unwise decisions I had made in my life. Those were some very dark days and I'm thankful that I was able to overcome.

I allowed all of the ups and downs we had been through in life to be my reason for holding on. One of my aunts told me, *"You young people don't have what it take nowadays to stick it out."* I remember saying to myself, if me sticking it out means enduring what you did, I don't want a marriage like that. Of course, those were my thoughts and I never verbalized those words, but it was the truth of how I felt. I didn't want a marriage that gave a false perception of love only because of the number of years we were together; when in reality I was in a living hell behind closed doors.

That evening after I said all I felt I was big and bad enough to say, I stormed off, grabbed a bag and packed some clothes. If he wasn't going to leave, then I would. That's when he went into the closet and took his gun off the top shelf. He never pointed it at me, and no words came out of his mouth, he just stood there with the gun at his side with his finger on the trigger as if he intended to use it. I knew at that moment we had reached a level that there was no turning back from. I silently said a prayer. I can't even recall all that I prayed, but afterwards, I do remember the next words out of my mouth to him were, *"You need help."* As I reflect on this statement, I say to myself, *"You needed just as much help as he did."*

As threatening as the situation was, there was a peace within me when I said those words. I don't know if it was the stillness in my voice or what, but he left the house that night and stayed gone for a few days. Very few people knew the events of that evening except my best friend and one of my aunts. I know both thought I was crazy for staying in the house and I'm sure they were furious with me. I knew that the marriage was over and I began to put my action plan into place. I had to leave and I did. This was over eight years ago.

The months and years after this wasn't easy at all. Everything around me seemed to be falling apart. The more I prayed, the more my life began to unravel. God was bringing discord to the things in my life that didn't belong. He was breaking me and setting me free from so many things. Although this is all clear to me now, during that time it wasn't.

Another Divine blessing that came out of this traumatic experience was court-ordered therapy. My ex contested the divorce. As a result, we both had to see a therapist together and individually. I thought to myself that this has got to be a joke. All the documented proof I had of the numerous affairs, threats and other things, how could a judge not automatically grant me a divorce? The truth of the matter is, had I not been ordered to seek a therapist, I may not have done it on my own. Even at such a low point in my life, God was in the midst, orchestrating it all.

In the beginning, I went to therapy with the attitude like let me hurry up and get through these sessions so I can be done with this. Little did I know it was in those sessions that my breakthrough would begin to take place. No longer was I focused on getting my point across for how I was the victim. The sessions really made me look deep into the core of how we both ended up in the various phases of our life. I'll never forget the exercises in which I had to discuss the foundation of my childhood, what that looked like and my experiences from it. Divine revelation of issues I had suppressed began to come to light.

Several months went by, therapy was going well and we both seemed to be in an amicable state. So much so, that I had even entertained the thought of reconciling, thinking we both were in a better place and could possibly try again. It didn't take long for certain behaviors to resurface and it was then that I knew brokenness is not something that is outgrown over time, it has to be healed. You can't heal what you aren't willing to face. I'm thankful it didn't take me another ten years to figure that out. In August 2012, after months of therapy, we both agreed the marriage was irreconcilable and the divorce was granted.

Healing is a process. The journey is not always easy. It is

freeing and liberating if you allow yourself to feel the very things you try to suppress. I learned my brokenness didn't start with the end of this marriage or the first one. I married the first time at a very young age. This marriage lasted a little over a year. That too was the result of where I was in my life; looking for love in all the wrong places and in the wrong people. The truth is I didn't even know how to love myself. In both marriages, I placed blame on my ex-spouses, when in actuality both mates were a reflection of the broken person I was. Today, I can honestly say I have released them from all the anger, hurt, bitterness and betrayal I felt they caused. I have also released myself from the role I played in allowing it to be.

I share my story because my experience has taught me there are many faces to domestic violence. I wasn't physically abused. So, I didn't associate the signs of control, manipulation, and being emotionally withdrawn as characteristics of domestic abuse. When I was in my teens, I watched my mother suffer as a victim of domestic abuse. I remember all too well that feeling of hopelessness; often wondering how she was going to protect us if she couldn't protect herself. While my sister's dad would physically abuse my mom, he abused me mentally and verbally. It was nothing for him to call me out of my name or make demeaning remarks to my brother and me.

The name calling and comments weren't all. There were

many acts of cruelty we endured by him. The day he was finally arrested and the secrets of what we had endured were finally exposed. I remember so vividly him calling me the "B" word to my face as the cops were hauling him off. For years, I felt the venom in his words. I knew that if he hadn't been detained, he probably would have tried to kill me. Even into my adult life, the days and nights of those years haunted me. I was so angry towards my mom. How could she let us go through this? Only to find myself repeating the same cycle. The thing is, I didn't recognize it as such because I didn't have the visible scars like she did.

Today I'm living in the truth of who I am, unapologetically. I'm thankful for the gift of resiliency. Without God's Divine grace and strength, I would not have made it through not only the divorce but the trauma endured in my childhood.

My experience has become my testimony. I have been afforded the opportunity through various platforms, to share my experience of how I have overcome. It is my hope that it will empower someone else looking for the strength needed to deal with their own crisis situation.

Please don't ever suffer in silence. There is nothing wrong with seeking professional help. I encourage it. God's Word promises that He'll give us beauty for ashes. I now know He allowed all of it so I could ultimately discover deeper mercy, kindness, love and unspeakable joy. The love I'm experiencing now and the amazing life-changing opportunities would not have been possible, had I not healed me first.

I never saw myself married again, and I was okay with that. In total transparency, I remember once telling myself that I've been down that road before and clearly it's not the road for me. Little did I know while God was healing and restoring me, He was preparing me for my Kingdom Purpose Mate and preparing him for me. On August 11, 2018, I said, *"I Do,"* to my very own prince charming. He protects me naturally and spiritually. He has helped me to truly understand that being vulnerable in love does not make you weak and being submissive doesn't mean losing yourself. He has supported me in healing every painful area of my life and lovingly embrace all of who I am; the good, bad and ugly. My soul is wealthy; but it was only until I did the work to heal everything. My life is every good and perfect gift God has promised that I'm to have and being Mrs. Stanback is just one of those gifts.

I'm thankful for the many life experiences for there was so much purpose in my pain. Six years ago, I launched a non-profit organization that provides support and resources to women in crisis situations. Having experienced various traumas of my own, I understand the need for a hand-up and not hand-out. It is for these reasons and many others, that I have a strong desire to create the same platform and sacred space for women to heal just as I have been given. Don't let the trauma detour your destiny, there is fullness of life on the other side if you trust the Source and the process; believing His plans are good for you.

ABOUT SHAUNTIA

Shauntia Stanback is the founder and Executive Director of Renewed Hope Life Center, a transitional and resource support center for women in crisis situations. She is very instrumental in her community and has sponsored numerous outreach initiatives that provide support and services to those in need.

Not knowing what her destiny would be, but trusting in God's word that His plans for her were good, Shauntia Wright persevered through her life challenges, and now uses her story to empower other women suffering in silence.

Shauntia has facilitated life skill training sessions and co-authored several self-help manuals that help women identify and overcome areas that keep them fearful and stuck.

She is now a certified Christian Life Coach (HIScoach), fully dedicated to helping others illuminate the greatness in them regardless of what the external circumstances look like.

Connect with Shauntia at www.facebook.com/shauntiaw

HE FASHIONED ME CLASSY

Tracey R. Wolfe

When you hear the word Classy, there are just some words that automatically come to mind: lady, poise, grace, elegance, and excellence. For as long as I can remember, being a Church girl has been synonymous with being a stylish dresser. Suits, gloves, heels, and hats were the norm and when you saw her, you knew she was a woman of style, distinction, and class. However, being classy is definitely not so much in the definition but in the behavior. The thought being that a woman's clothing was a reflection of her character.

Merriam-Webster defines Classy as elegant, stylish, having or reflecting high standards of personal behavior, and admirable, skillful, and graceful. Other definitions of classy include: stylish, high-class, superior, exclusive, chic, elegant, smart, sophisticated, upscale, upmarket, high-toned, posh, ritzy, plush, swanky, styling/stylin', decent, gracious, respectable, and noble. I can honestly say these adjectives describe me very well, but the word classy means so much more to me.

My personal definition of classy:

A trailblazer with poise and grace, having standards in every area of your life, striving for excellence, having a spirit of hospitality, treating everyone with respect. Being marvelous, bold, unique not arrogant, yet confident in who God has called you to be.

Regardless if you have on a $2000.00 St. John® suit, with Jimmy Choo® high heeled shoes, or if you have on a T-shirt, flop flips, and a pair of jeans, you can still be considered classy. How a woman acts, expresses herself verbally and non-verbally, and lives her life are some of the distinctions of whether she is classy or not.

Growing up to be classy was the farthest thing from my mind, because I was trying so hard to fit in. In the midst of wanting to fit in, I didn't realize how blessed I was as a young girl. I didn't understand that I was wonderfully made and that God was protecting me from a lifestyle that He never wanted me to experience, but a destiny He wanted me to cherish.

"What would you say to your younger self?" As a motivational speaker, I get asked this question quite frequently. Depending on

how much time I have, my answer may be short and sweet with just two words, *"A lot!"* I have so much knowledge now, here are a few words of wisdom I would share with my younger self. (1) There is nothing wrong with being different. Go. Do. Be. Go where God wants you to go. Do what God wants you to do and be who God has created you to be. (2) Trust the process. No one likes the developmental stages of each level of becoming, but everyone loves the results. However, on the other side of the process is a greater you. (3) God made you! Be the best you. Don't be anyone else but you. Stay in your lane and exercise your God given gifts to be the best version of you that you can be.

Being Classy Means Being Different

"I will praise thee; for I am fearfully and wonderfully made: marvelous are thy works; and that my soul knoweth right well."
(Psalm 139:14, KJV)

God made each one of us different. We each have a purpose in life. No two people are the same, not even twins. We are uniquely made for a specific reason and we have our own challenges and trials that create a personal testimony.

I wanted to be light-skinned. I wanted to be skinny. I wanted to make A's every semester in every class. I thought that being a perfectionist was a horrific thing. I wanted to be everything I wasn't but God did have a plan for my life.

Growing up, I wanted to be the kid that made straight A's in every class, however academics just did not come easy to me. Even with tutoring and extra credit, I still did not excel like I desired. I was dealing with peer pressure and coupled with having challenges with school work, I became critical of myself which put a strain on my teenage years. As a result, I developed a perfectionist complex. I felt as if everything had to be done perfectly and if it wasn't perfect, it wasn't good enough. I set unrealistic expectations for myself and when I couldn't measure up to them, I felt like a failure. At that time I didn't know what I know now – I was a perfectionist. As a perfectionist, not making good grades bothered me when I was younger. Today, I realize that Christ is the only perfect being and that because I am human, it's ok to make mistakes. I strive to be the best me I can be, however, I understand I am not perfect.

In 2000, I graduated Carolina Beauty College as valedictorian with my cosmetology licenses. For the first time, I was academically where I wanted to be. That feeling of accomplishment was one of the best I have ever experienced. Graduating top of my class and delivering the valedictorian speech – just reminiscing about that moment still makes my heart flutter.

Right out of beauty school, I worked at one of the most

luxurious Salon & Day Spas in North Carolina, which further enhanced my skills and professionalism. I gained confidence in my craft, stepped out on faith, and opened my own salon. I made sure every beauty service I performed was with love and every client's beauty desires were met with excellence. Within a few years, I evolved and started a Bling T-Shirt and accessories online business. I handpick each accessory and I make sure each custom t-shirt is flawless before the order leaves the studio.

Today, I have turned those negative thoughts about being a perfectionist into a positive outlook on life. I used being a perfectionist to my advantage. Instead of trying to live up to unrealistic expectations, I simply strive to be a better person than I was yesterday.

There is nothing wrong with being different. What I thought was a struggle was only a stepping stone into my greatness.

Being Classy Is an Inner Work – Trust the Process

"Your beauty should not come from outward adornment, such as elaborate hairstyles and the wearing of gold jewelry or fine clothes. Rather, it should be that of your inner self, the unfading beauty of a gentle and quiet spirit, which is of great worth in God's sight"
(1 Peter 3:3-4, NIV).

I lived with my mother and father who were, and still are,

Holy-Ghost spirit filled, fire baptized, running for the Lord and haven't gotten tired yet, Baptist Christians. I said all that to say I grew up in a household that had lots of rules and standards. Of course as a child, I didn't understand the rules nor did I like them. As a young adult, I rebelled and did some crazy and shameful things. However, as an adult, I praise God for every rule and standard my parents set for me because they knew what was best. They could see things I couldn't see. I had no clue they were being guided by God to raise me up to become the lady I am today. This is why I take parenting so seriously. I see the importance of parental guidance. The best advice my mom gave me, *"Always put God first."*

In 2016, I wrote an e-book entitled, *"Eight Ways To Raising Them Better Not Bitter"*. The e-book is a personal testimony of how I applied those eight methods and created a peaceful and nourishing relationship with my children. As a woman who has been divorced twice, I can honestly say I was becoming bitter. I was so bitter, I plotted to end my own life as well as those who had hurt me. I saw how my negative disposition was affecting my beautiful daughters. It wasn't until I applied what my Pastor taught me about faith and letting go of the past to my everyday life that I began to see changes in myself. As a parent, I had to pull it together. God guided me on becoming a better person. I had no idea that He wanted me to become an author, yet when I said yes to His voice, I began to heal. As a parent, I truly understand the process that I had to take, not only for myself, but for my children, my children's children, and everyone God has called me to touch.

As an Image Coach, I teach on inner and outer beauty because what's on the inside shows up on the outside. Dressing nice is only one half of the whole picture. A stylish exterior coupled with spreading the love of God with others, that's classy. You can have on the cheapest outfit, however, when God's light shines through you, you will look like a million bucks.

Being Classy Means Being the Best You God Made You to Be!

"Beloved, I wish above all things that thou mayest prosper and be in health, even as thy soul prospereth"
(3 John 2, KJV).

I must admit, I love to look nice. I have always had a passion for fashion. My hair always looked great and I always wore the latest styles of clothing. On the flip side, I always struggled with my weight. Despite my fondness for sharp dressing, I still never thought I looked good enough. My mother went on diets with me. She exercised with me trying to get the weight off but my weight went up and down like a yo-yo. Once I got in high school

I realized I was an emotional eater. I really didn't get victory over my weight challenges until I was married and had my daughters.

One day I said to my daughters, *"Y'all gettin' thick."* One of them replied back, *"Mom, you thick."* That statement changed my life. It opened my eyes to the image of me I thought they were seeing but they actually weren't. I had an image of the me I wanted others to see and I felt I needed to make some changes right away. I started researching healthy eating options, different body types, and what exercises were best for me as a pear shaped woman. God created me, so I decided to be the best 5' 2" pear shape me I could be.

I now help other men and women with their weight issues and body flaw insecurities. As a Personal Shopper, I also assist people with their wardrobe and what looks best on their body type. God desires us to be prosperous physically, spiritually, and financially. He created all of us for His purpose so, I admonish you to be the best you.

In all of my experiences, I have learned to live life intentionally. With God's strength, I am able to do everything that He has called me to do. Sometimes I sit back and laugh because at one time in my life, speaking in public was terrifying to me. Don't get me wrong I still get butterflies, yet now I do not turn down the opportunity to provoke men, women, boys, and girls to keep shining everyday regardless of their life's circumstances. It gives me great joy knowing that I am doing the will of God and blessing someone's life with His Word and my life journey.

We all have our triumphs and challenges. God ordained it that way so everyone will have their own personal testimony. Becoming who God wants you to be doesn't happen overnight, however, I have learned to embrace and be at peace with who I am called to be. With all my imperfections and the mistakes I have made, I count it all joy. I love the lady God made me and I'm loving the skin I'm in. I am a C.H.U.R.C.H. Girl unapologetically. I wasn't destined to fit in. I was born to shine and be who God has called me to be – CLASSY!

ABOUT TRACEY

Tracey R. Wolfe is a native of Winston-Salem North Carolina. She is the owner of Flawless Image-Beauty-Fashion where her passion is coaching people on their inner and outer beauty, and helping individuals with their personal brand and professional image development. As Chief Executive Officer of TRW Management, Tracey and her professional staff manage people, events & small businesses with excellence.

Tracey serves as a member of the Piedmont Triad Women's Forum, corporate partner with Dress to Success and is on the Board of Directors for Phenomenal Woman, an organization which ministers to battered women. She is the author of *"8 Ways to Raising Them to be Better Not Bitter"* and is a part of numerous mentoring programs & outreach ministries. She is also the proud mother of two beautiful daughters. Tracey's mission is to empower men, women, boys and girls to Keep Shining 365 regardless of their circumstances!

Connect with Tracey at www.keepshining365.com.

You Can't Take My Oil

Cassandra Elliott

I really don't know where to begin. As I sit here, the first thought that comes to mind is the fact that a lot of people were mad at God on my behalf. They love me so much that they asked God, *"Hasn't she been through enough?"* They knew they didn't have a monopoly on what life events happened to me, however, they just, like me, couldn't understand how it was that I survived life threatening kidney disease to end up here.

I'll begin by telling you how it was that I received some not so great news in the most insensitive way possible. I was in the doctor's office, having come back for a follow up of some test results. The door opens. The nurse comes in the room, hands me an envelope that says IT'S CANCER, and walks out of the room. No empathy and no bedside manner whatsoever. Just me in a room in a pink robe waiting for the pathology of a biopsy from 24 hours before.

When she left the room, I turned to my loving husband of twenty years, Bryant, bury my head in his chest, and scream. He wiped the tears from my eyes and helped me get dressed. I managed to pull myself together and shift my composure because I had to walk through the waiting room passed others who were waiting just like I was to receive their news one way or another. Once I got in the car, the tears began to flow again as I began to make the phone calls to relay the news to the rest of my family.

Why am I here again? When did this happen? Why did this happen? Why is this happening again? I remember the day I came off the stage after leading worship. I put my hand on my right breast and there was a lump – a small lump that was not there earlier that morning. When I mentioned it, someone's response was not to worry about it and they went through their barrage of uncertifiable diagnoses that added up to nothing in their minds. Thus, I ignored it and continued to travel and do ministry only to notice it was getting larger and larger. It was so large that it began to become painfully uncomfortable to simply lift my hands. The lump was so heavy it could not be ignored. As I traveled different places to minister, I requested prayer from those I trusted. The Word of the Lord to me was that this affliction was not unto death. I received the word of the Lord while the lump was still growing.

No longer able to ignore it, I paid a visit to my gynecologist. He said to me emphatically, *"It cannot be cancer!"* He knew my history and just could not believe or, let me say, would not believe that it was cancer. He gave me instructions to go to the breast center and have them take a needle and pull out the fluid as he was sure this was all it was. I followed his instructions and made the appointment only to get there and find out that whatever this was, was in the tissue of my breast. There was no fluid. There was nothing to pull out.

As a worshipper, I knew what I needed to do and that was to gather together those that loved me to seek God with me and pray me through this. You've got to be so careful who you invite into your intimate life situations. You've got to know who to trust. Proverbs 81:21 says, *"Death and life are in the power of the tongue..."* and I couldn't have anything spoken over my life other than what the Lord had already said: THIS AFFLICTION IS NOT UNTO DEATH! This gathering together was not about sharing my issue as gossip. It was about people coming together to worship with me, to believe with me, to agree with me that this was not my end, and that I would be healed.

I sent out invitations to those that I knew would come and worship. My spiritual mother took the lead and instructed everyone, *"This is not the time to cry. This is not the time not to have faith.*

This is not the time to draw from Cassandra. This is the time to pour into her and to believe in faith for her deliverance." We crafted a prayer and named the issue in the prayer and prayed at it together for twenty-one days. Lady Thursday sat on the wall worshipping quietly. After some time she said, *"I don't propose to be a prophet but I hear in my spirit, this will not be a long journey."* I was so thankful for her obedience and the word she released to me in that moment. It gave me hope and strength that God was thinking about me.

The day finally came for us to travel to the cancer center for testing and to meet my oncologist. He was an interesting man with an interesting face, interesting hair, and in a definitely interesting atmosphere. My sister-in-law, Gloria, my brother-in-law, Clarence, Lady Thursday, and Sandy accompanied me along with my husband. This was not the time to face this alone. They sat praying with us.

The first day was so scary. I actually saw the scan of the lump. It was so large. The doctor looked at it and didn't know what to say. Gloria and Sandy looked at it and didn't know what to say. They held my hands as I screamed aloud. I cried, *"God this cannot be happening to me! Why me? Where did this come from?"* They not only held my hands, they cried with me.

Once I was able to pull myself together, the doctor gave me the course of action. It was to shrink, radiate, and rebuild. In my mind's eye, I could not believe this was what God wanted for me.

The doctor, then, told me they were going to try chemotherapy as well. He said I would lose my hair by the second treatment and my life would never be the same again. What do you do when you have faith to believe that what they have diagnosed you with is not your portion nor your promise?

In every trial, there are moments that define what you and what you're going through. When the doctor told me that I was going to lose my hair, I refuted his words and I looked at him and said, *"I will not lose my hair!"* I emphatically said to him, *"I will not lose my hair!"* However, reflecting back to the day I was taking out my braids to have my hair rebraided was an emotional one. I was home alone. My husband was working and as I sat waiting for the young lady to show up, I touched one of the braids and it fell out in my hand! I said to myself, *"It's just a loose braid."* As I went to touch the next braid, it fell as well. I started screaming, *"No, no, not my hair!"* I reached for my phone and dialed the last number in my log. All the way to Houston Texas, the unsuspecting sister answered the phone to hear me screaming to the top of my lungs! She was trying to make sense of what she was hearing, however, at first, all she could ask was, *"What's wrong, what's the matter?"* Finally, in a voice she could make out, she heard me cry, *"My hair, my hair is falling out! My hair!"* I screamed and I cried and I screamed and I cried. She told me to hang up so that she could call someone to come to me because she was in Texas and couldn't get to me right away. In what seemed like about five minutes time, Mama Shaw was at the door. I just sat at the table with the hair in my hand. I her efforts to console me, she just held me and prayed for me. To this day, I still have the hair.

Afterwards, I had to make the decision to completely cut off my hair. I was grateful for how much support I had and how much love I was shown. These are the moments when you are going through crisis and trusting God that you hope those who say they love you really show up. Kala Slade is the owner of Simply Beautiful Salon which she closed down just for me to invite my sisters and my friends. They were all strong for me because of what we were about to experience. As I lay my head back in the bowl, Mama Shaw stood in front of me so that I could focus on her. Lawana prayed at my feet praying and Dee held my hand. My sisters that own their own salons had scissors in their hands as I had tears in my eyes.

As they washed my hair, they began to worship. While worship music played and I was trusting God in that moment because I knew when my head came back out of the shampoo bowl I would have no hair. I kept praying for the Lord to give me strength and courage. Lord give me strength and courage, I repeated over and over again. Dee held my hand and she said, *"You've got to write this song."* In the next moment, Mama Shaw's faced shifted and I knew something was wrong. She looked at me and said, *"Just focus on me, we got you."* What I later learned was that my hair was falling out at the root because of the chemicals that were in my body. There was no need for additional scissors. When it was time to lift my head out of the shampoo bowl, I was so afraid to look at myself. However, everyone assured me that I was still beautiful. My barber came as well to make sure that I left feeling beautiful. Afterwards I was presented with a beautiful sequined winged scarf. This sealed everything that had taken place on that day and left me well prepared to continue my journey.

Finally it was December and I was preparing for my final chemo treatment. Because of everything I had been going through, I decided I was going to cancel my yearly worship, The Gathering. I didn't want people to see me in my current state. I was completely bald, weak, and tired. However, just as I was making the preparations to cancel, I heard the Lord say, *"Don't cancel. Create a place for people who are going through what you're going through but didn't believe me for their healing. What you desire for yourself, desire it for others and call it Healing Worship."* I was obedient to the Lord, but because I knew that I needed strength to stand and minister, we postponed the last chemo treatment. That night, I lost my voice. I was weak and tired from my chemo treatments. But to see people at the altar calling on the name of Jesus for healing, deliverance, and relief was all worth it. The presence of God filled that place. Many received more than just physical healing but emotional, spiritual, family healing, reconciliation, and restoration.

I was January 2014. I was very aware that my treatment was coming to its end and I was fully prepared to ring that Bell, walk out of that place, and never come back. Even though the doctor said there would be a possibility that I would need radiation, I still believed I was healed and that all of this ordeal was over.

When I went back for my first post chemo visit, I found out my first doctor had been released and I had a brand new doctor. At first I thought, *"Oh Lord, what now?"* I believe that when God is doing something new, He does it right in front of you because He needs you to have a front row seat to the miracle He's getting ready to perform in your life. The doctor looked at my chart and it seemed at first he thought he saw something, but then it disappeared. He took a second look and said, *"Wow! you are clear and clean!"* You know I sat there waiting for the ball to drop – that I needed a radiology. He looked at me and simply said, *"You're clean. Have a good day and I'll see you again at your next appointment"* and he walked out of the room. Mama Shaw and I sat there speechless. After a while, I realized what had just happened. He had confirmed the healing that had taken place in my body and I was ever so grateful. I slowly stood up, gathered my belongings, and walked out of the room with a praise on my lips and a praise in my heart. God had done it once again.

I've been through too much not to worship Him is not just a lyric to a song for me, it is my life. I am a living testimony, I am a miracle, and I am healed!

ABOUT CASSANDRA

Pastor Cassandra Elliott, also known as the "Purpose Pusher" and the "Giant Slayer" is a walking example of the Five-Fold Ministry. A native of New York City, Cassandra began playing music at a young age; this passion unfolded into accepting the call as a Pastor of Worship, teaching the Word of God, and becoming an innovator and mentor to many. She is a survivor of Kidney Disease and Breast Cancer and has used both of these testimonies as a vehicle to encourage others through the preached, taught and imparted Word of God.

Currently residing in Greensboro, NC with her husband Bryant Elliott of 25 years, Pastor Elliott leaves her testimony and the words of Philippians 1:6 to those who are also weathering storms and waiting on God: *"Remember that He, who hath begun a good work in you, will perform it until the day of Jesus Christ."*

Connect with Cassandra at www.cassandraelliott.com.

With His Stripes I Am Healed

Alberta Gail Wright

Hebrews 12:1 says, *"Now faith is the substance of things hoped for, the evidence of things not seen."* My story is just that, a story of faith. It began in August of 2000 when I was diagnosed with Multiple Sclerosis. MS is a chronic, progressive disease of the central nervous system that disturbs the flow of communication from the brain to the body. There are several symptoms that cause this disease including numbness or tingling, speech problems, muscle weakness, loss of coordination, blurred vision, trembling, memory loss, and severe fatigue to name a few. I have experienced all of these symptoms and more, however, with these symptoms plaguing my body, I have, also, experienced miraculous healing in my body and I continue to trust and believe God for total healing.

When I was diagnosed with MS, I was seeing a neurologist that had been treating me for muscle spasms. I had a car accident and he thought the shaking I was experiencing in my arm came from muscle spasms, however, they began to get more and more severe. The shaking progressed from my arm to my whole body. The doctor's prognosis was that I was having seizures and that I should start seizure medicine immediately. I know doctors are supposed to be the experts but everything in my spirit kept telling me it was not a seizure.

The neurologist sent me to have an electroencephalogram, a test used to find problems related to electrical activity of the brain. While I was laying on the table, I whispered a prayer, *"Lord, please let me have a spasm on this table to prove I am not having seizures."* They started the machine and told me not to move, however, no sooner than the test began, I had a violent spasm. When it finally stopped, the nurse confirmed what I felt in my spirit all along, that what I was experiencing complete muscle spasms and not seizures. The doctor was completely baffled. He sent me to the University of Pennsylvania to have further testing with another neurologist there.

When I arrived at the UOP appointment, they completed further testing and a full blood workup. They also did an MRI of my brain. When the results came back, the diagnosis was Multiple Sclerosis. The nurse I had was a Godsend. She pulled me to the side and said to me, *"Mrs. Wright, I fear your previous neurologist has misdiagnosed you. I am glad we have been able to provide you with the correct diagnosis before he started you on a course of medication that could have been detrimental for you!"* Well, you know I left out of that office praising God. I know you're confused. I'd just received a diagnosis for a degenerative disease that there is no cure for. It wasn't that I didn't hear the diagnosis, what mattered more to me was the fact that I knew I heard from God and the same God that assured me I was not having seizures was the same God who would deliver me from this diagnosis!

Armed with my praise, I returned to the doctor who sent me to the University of Pennsylvania. By now he had received the results and his conversation was not uplifting to say the least. He looked at me and said, *"Mrs. Wright, the results of which I know you were told already but it looks like you have Multiple Sclerosis."* Then he said, *"You know that you're going to live with this the rest of your life."* He continued with his "you'll nevers" and his "you'll always," however, I began to speak Isaiah 54:17, *"No weapon that is formed against thee shall prosper; and every tongue that shall rise against thee in judgment thou shalt condemn. This is the heritage of the servants of the Lord, and their righteousness is of me, saith the Lord."* I told the Lord I was going to stand on His Word. I had received the doctor's report but I chose to believe the report of the Lord. His report said by His stripes, I am healed! *"But he was wounded for our transgressions, he was bruised for our iniquities: the chastisement of our peace was upon him; and with his stripes we are healed" (Isaiah 53:5, KJV)*. I never stepped foot back into that doctor's office again. I knew death and life was in the power of the tongue and I was not agreement with the death sentence he was trying to prescribe for my life!

A month later, I began to experience more symptoms from the MS diagnosis and I started losing my eyesight. By the end of that month, I could no longer even read my bible. I had started at the School of Ministry and fear quickly set in that I wouldn't be able to complete my studies because I couldn't see. However, God had another plan! My girlfriend, Lynn, bought me cassette tapes of the Bible that I was able to listen to and use to complete my school work. Even though I couldn't read it, I could hear it, which further fueled my faith. *"So then faith cometh by hearing, and hearing by the word of God," (Romans 10:17, KJV)*.

From September to December, I was still experiencing muscle spasms, yet, during that time my relationship with God got even closer. The more I listened to the Word of God, the more the Word came alive in my life. I particularly focused on healing scriptures. I meditated on Isaiah 53:5 day and night along with books I purchased about the healing power of God. I stood steadfast on God's Word because I knew it possessed the power to heal me. Then it happened!

December 14, 2012 I was home alone. For months and

months I was experiencing muscle spasms that were getting progressively worse. I could be sitting and my arms would just start shaking. I had fallen several times because I had no control of my legs. I had a muscle spasm so severe that it curled me up in a fetal position. My body was writhing in pain and all I could do was call on the name of Jesus. Over and over again, I called on the name of Jesus. We say all the time, something happens when you call on the name of Jesus but that day, laying on the floor in a fetal position, unable to uncurl my arms and legs in excruciating pain, Jehovah Rapha, the Lord my healer showed up! In just a few minutes later, the pain stopped and my body uncurled itself and I haven't had a spasm since!

I moved to North Carolina in October 2013. When I left New Jersey, I received specific instructions to have an MRI of my brain every year to see if any lesions returned in my brain or if my condition had worsened. Two years before we moved, I had missed seeing the neurologist so when I first saw my new doctor, he ordered another MRI of my brain. When I went back for the results the doctor said, *"Mrs. Wright, I have good news and I have bad news."*

I told her, *"If it's all the same to you, I'd like the bad news first."*

So she said, *"The bad news is that while we were doing your MRI, you stopped breathing ten times. This is an indication that you have sleep apnea and you need to sleep with a c-pap machine to regulate your breathing."*

This time I was the one who was baffled.

I said, *"That's the bad news?"* I was actually thinking she was going to tell me something I didn't want to hear. I didn't tell her but I had stopped taking my medication. There were times when I went to take it and I distinctly heard the Holy Spirit tell me not to. (Disclaimer: I am not advocating that you stop taking your doctor prescribed medications. Always consult with your doctor before discontinuing any medication prescribed by your doctor. *"Wisdom is the principle thing; therefore get wisdom: and with all thy getting get understanding" (Proverbs 4:7, KJV).*

"Yes ma'am. Now for the good news. I have the results from the MRI we took of your brain last week. I compared it to the one you had three years ago and I am quite shocked. What have you been doing?"

I asked, *"What do you mean?"* I was honest and told her that I had stopped taking my medication and why.

She said, *"The MRI from last week shows the left side of your brain completely intact unlike the one from three years ago which show the lesions on your brain. These results show your brain is completely healed."* I tell you, I give God the glory today because I know my healing came from nobody but God. I know that I am a living testimony to show forth the marvelous works of the Lord.

I've battled many afflictions in my body. I have been affected in almost every place in my body from the top of my head to the soles of my feet – BUT GOD! I held on to His Word that says,

"Many are the afflictions of the righteous: but the Lord delivereth him out of them ALL!" (Psalm 34:19, KJV). Everything I've been through has brought me closer to the Lord and taught me valuable principles that I carry with me daily to help me be an even greater witness for the Lord.

First, I learned to stand on His Word no matter what the doctor's reports said or what the situation looked like. God's Word is the most important substance for our healing. *"God means what he says. What he says goes. His powerful Word is sharp as a surgeon's scalpel, cutting through everything, whether doubt or defense, laying us open to listen and obey. Nothing and no one is impervious to God's Word. We can't get away from it—no matter what" (Ephesians 4:12, MSG)*. I learned to never accept anything contrary to the Word of God. Words have power and if we believe the wrong set of words, we risk falling victim to a mindset that puts us in bondage. If we accept the wrong set of words, we risk accepting a fate over our lives that Christ never ordained. We have power over every situation through the Word of God.

Second, I learned as people of God, we go through afflictions, it's not about us. We go through so that we can help somebody else. *"And they overcame him by the blood of the Lamb, and by the word of their testimony; and they loved not their lives unto the death" (Revelation 12:11, KJV)*. Most times we blame God when we go through things not understanding that He chose us because He trusts that what He already put in us is enough to get us through. After we get through it, we have a track record with the Lord we can share with others that will help them overcome. For example, one day my friend Belinda was very heavy in my spirit. When I called her to see how she was doing, she told me that it was truly the Lord who had her call me. She was on the verge of ending her life because she was so tired of suffering. I prayed with her and encouraged her not to give up but to keep trusting God.

Finally, I learned how truly important it is to have a relationship with the Lord and to remain faithful and consistent attending church services regularly. *"And let us consider how we may spur one another on toward love and good deeds, not giving up meeting together, as some are in the habit of doing, but encouraging one another—and all the more as you see the Day approaching"* (Hebrews 10:25, NIV). When we experience life challenges, the first thing we often do is stay home and lock ourselves away from the support system that will help us get through it all. I received Jesus Christ as Lord and Savior of my life at age fourteen at a Vacation Bible School. I haven't been perfect, yet I have served Him faithfully since that time. I have been blessed with wonderful pastors, Bishop Freddy Washington and Bishop Kevin A. Williams, who preached me through some of my most difficult times. I had two bad relapses last year. Bishop Williams was teaching on healing during that time. I was able to fortify myself even more in the Word of God, the prayers of the righteous, and the strength that comes from fellowshipping with the people of God. I am a C.H.U.R.C.H. Girl, a proud witness for Christ, and I give Him all the glory for all He has done in my life.

About Alberta Gail

Alberta Gail Wright was born and raised in Salem, New Jersey. She accepted the Lord Jesus as her savior and was baptized at the age of fourteen.

She married the late Joseph William Wright, Sr. in 1977. To this union, two children were born: Senica Lynn and Joseph William Wright, Jr. Gail is the proud grandparent of four grandchildren and four great-grandchildren.

Gail served as a CNA and clerk for sixteen years at Salem Memorial Hospital. She graduated in 2010 from Jameson School of Theology with an Evangelistic License.

Gail served as a Deaconess at the WORD Church under the leadership of Bishop Freddy Washington until her journey to High Point, North Carolina in 2013. She is currently a member of Monument of Praise Church under the leadership of Dr. Kevin A. Williams.

Gail, blessed with the gift of song, has ministered in music alongside her sisters, The Cline Sisters, for the past twenty years. They were blessed to do their first live recording in April 2018. She sings in the Ensemble and G.G.O (God's Gift in Operation) choirs at her church and her favorite scripture is Isaiah 53:5, *"But he was wounded for our transgressions, he was bruised for our iniquities: the chastisement of our peace was upon him; and with his stripes we are healed."*

This is My Story, This is My Song

Robin V. Yelverton

When I think of my story, there is much that comes to my mind. However, what I'm about to share began a very important period in my life. It's when I really began to walk with God.

I got married way early — age eighteen to be exact. I had my first child at twenty and number two child at twenty-two. I strived hard to keep my family together and many times it was just my children and I. I can remember while I was in the midst of trying to raise my children, be a wife and grow up myself, I begin to quickly realize that I couldn't do it without God. I really needed Him and I needed to know Him for myself, not through the eyes and testimonies of other people. Realizing what I had to do for my life as well as the life of my family, I decided to find out for myself who and what God was really all about and not relying on what others had to say.

Being separated from my husband at the time, I was working and taking care of my children alone. Each day we would come home, get homework done, have dinner, get baths and go to bed. After the kids went to bed, I would sit in my chair in my room and there I began to read the Word of God. I made up in my mind that even if I didn't understand what I was reading, I would read it anyway and that's exactly what I did. As I read my word daily and prayed to the Lord, that Word started to jump off the pages and things began to happen in my life, some strange things at that. I started experiencing God's voice speaking to me and through me. It scared me sometimes because I would hear it and look around thinking, *"Who said that? I know I'm in this room by myself."* Some would say I was crazy saying God spoke to me however, if you've never had the pleasure of experiencing his voice, oh well!!

Late one night I was in a deep sleep and suddenly I was awakened. I opened my eyes and looked around. I started to get up and was literary pushed down in my bed by my shoulders and I felt something or someone sitting on my feet, then a hand went around my neck chocking me. I couldn't move. I could only move my eyes back and forth. For a minute, I couldn't speak. I just barely got out the words, *"The Blood of Jesus!"* I kept saying it and shortly that spirit let go. I jumped out of my bed, walked through the house, and commanded that spirit to leave my house. I walked through my kids rooms and spoke the Word of God over them. I walked to the kitchen, opened the back door, and commanded that spirit to get out. This was my first encounter with spiritual warfare.

As time went on I could feel myself getting stronger in the Lord but the enemy never gives up. His sole purpose is to kill, steal, and destroy. Three years after I divorced my first husband, I married again. This experience was another level. Why do I say this? Because I told the Lord, if I meet a man who is in love with Him, I figured I wouldn't have to worry if he would be in love with me. Now I believe that he did love God, but there were some issues that were not revealed. We all have them. Some we are just not currently aware of. However, I've learned some very important things. We all grow up differently and have different home lives and those things impact us as we and become adults. If you grew up in a home where there was discord and dysfunction, alcohol addiction, abuse, etc., or in a home that was the opposite; no discord, or fighting, both scenarios have an impact on your life.

I grew up in a home where there was no fighting. I'm sure

my parents had issues and problems between them but, as a child growing up, I never knew it because they never displayed that in front of myself or my siblings. I never saw them fight. I never saw or heard my Mom disrespect my Dad or my Dad disrespect my Mom in anyway. Speaking of my Mom, she taught me so much; she was a strong woman, thus her maiden name, Strong. She was short in stature and my Dad often called her shorty, but she rose tall in her acts of kindness and she was full of wisdom. She taught me how to be a lady and more than that, a Godly woman. She spoke out on things and issues without hesitation. There was no guessing about her. You knew exactly where she stood and she did it with grace.

It was good for me to see a husband and wife operate the way my parents did because it was a testament that it could be done. However, it impacted my life in a way that left me wanting because it wasn't my reality. So, when faced with these issues, I didn't know how to respond or how to deal with any of it. I didn't know how to deal with conflict or controversy or how to address someone who wasn't truthful, like I said I took people at their word. I didn't experience the Friday night knock down drag out fighting and I wasn't familiar with someone coming in drunk. I didn't experience the verbal abuse and the mental abuse that was just as bad. I was totally out of my league.

We were married for twenty five years. We became a blended family; he had three kids and I had two. We joined our families and raised our kids together. I took his kids as my own and tried again to hold our family together. However I had no idea how differently we were raised and how much of an impact it would have on our lives and marriage.

During those years, I had so many challenges. On a good note, I know how strong your marriage can be when two walk together and more than that, when the two can pray together. Despite his other shortcomings, I was married to a man who had the gift of faith and lived by that. Like I said we grew up differently. I watched my Mom take care of the household, take care of my siblings, my Dad, and myself. This is not heard of in the 21st century because so many women now work outside the home. My mom worked briefly outside of the home when I was very young. She pushed my sisters and I to be independent, get jobs, and work hard. She never learned how to drive herself but she insisted that we all get our licenses.

After twenty-five years of marriage, kids all grown up, married with grandkids coming, the man I thought I would spend the rest of my life with was no longer the man for my life. Throughout our marriage there was infidelity, lies, disrespect, mental and sexual abuse. I never shared this with anyone other than my doctor who insisted I have an HIV test every time I went for my yearly office visit. It was a bit much for me, but I knew she was doing her job.

He had a pattern that, after some time, I figured out. He would get involved with women casually through conversation and then things would progress. I believe he would realize what he had gotten into before he would stop. I began to realize the differences in his behavior after each encounter. That's how I was able to figure things out – mainly because he would treat me crazy after it was over. I figured it out a little late for myself, but they say better late than never. One of his encounters left a woman pregnant. She came to my home to talk to him. He wouldn't even go to the door and talk to her. He just left her outside until she left. According to her, she lost her baby after seven months of pregnancy.

The mental abuse was overwhelming and I didn't realize how much it was taking a toll on me, physically and mentally. It's not like I didn't know where this was headed. The Lord had already spoken to me but you know how you try to dismiss the Lord speaking to you. Had I listened, I may have prevented so much heartache in my life. The final blow came after we lost our home and ended up in a place we never should have been. As his disrespect became more blatant, I realized I needed to make my move.

I found a townhouse and did just that, moved. This move was so very difficult because I had gotten used to a partner and not being alone. Even with our dysfunction, I thought I had someone to share with every day and build a future with after twenty-five years or so I thought. I lived each day with uncertainty; living with someone but lonely, bruised and hurting. The last three years were the worst and I had no idea how much stress I was under. After years of trying to hold it all together, pretending life was good, and trying to fit a circle in a square peg, the heavy weight of it all came crashing in like a tsunami on November 20, 2015.

Early that morning around 3 a.m., I could not rest. I couldn't lie down flat and was very short of breath. I felt strongly that I needed to call 911. When the ambulance arrived, they took my vitals, checked me and said that they would be taking me out. However, they never told me what the problem was! After being assisted into the ambulance, the driver asked me which hospital I wanted to go to. Before I could respond, the EMS who was a lady said, *"We're taking her to Durham."* First, I thought to myself, "Why are they asking me what hospital when the closest hospital is only two exits down?" My next thought was, *"I can't be that bad if they're going to drive me to a hospital that is thirty to forty minutes away."* This, however, was the farthest from the truth. It was *really* bad. Once we arrived at the hospital, I was immediately taken me to the Cath Lab where they began working on me. The last thing I remember is the nurses getting me hooked up to IV's.

Five days later, I woke up in the ICU. When I opened my eyes, my son walked over to my bed and looked down at me. I lifted my hand and he grabbed it. I had tubes everywhere and a trach in my neck so I couldn't speak. He said, *"Mom, do you know what happened?"* I shook my head no. He began telling me what had transpired in the last five days. As he spoke, tears began to roll down my face.

What happened? I had been in a coma for five days and the day I woke up was before Thanksgiving. I went into cardiac arrest! The doctor was in such a hurry to get stents into my heart, he ruptured the femoral artery in my leg. From that point, they had to cut me open and during this process they lacerated my liver. They first came out and told my family that I may lose my leg because of the ruptured artery. However, I DIED! Yes, I flatlined right there on the table. They came out and told my family I didn't make it! But God had other plans! (Ok, every time I share this, I have to pause just to worship!) They managed to revive me! Yes, I was brought back to life! After I was revived, they told my family if I made it pass forty-eight hours, I had a chance. One of my church mothers said to me, *"Baby, the devil intended to kill you but the Holy Trinity showed up!"* That's why I'm still here!

After a few days they pulled me out bed and sat me up in a chair. Sitting up one morning, a guy came in my room and introduced himself. He was one of the nurses that had cared for me while I was in a coma. He kneeled down on his knees, grabbed my hand, and said to me, *"I know you don't remember me."* With tears in his eyes, he continued, *"I just had to come see how you were doing and to tell you, You are a miracle!"* Tears fells from my eyes and his. I thought to myself, *"Something happened in that room that impacted this man's life so much that he came back just to let me know he felt he has witnessed a miracle!"* God is so absolutely awesome! He is the God of the whole earth!

So very much happened to me during this pivotal turn in my life. It was months before I could remember what happened to me and still today, there are some things that occurred that have not come back to my remembrance. I truly believe the Lord just blocked it out.

When you're a child of God, you are anointed and have a calling on your life (and we all do, just on different levels), the enemy knows it. Your attacks come on a whole different level. He came at me with loaded barrels. I am sure of the person that came through this on the other side because I am Chosen, Holy, Unique (I don't fit in and I'm cool with that), Resilient, (I went through it, I survived it, and I'm still here). Classy (I'm Carrie's Girl), and Healed, (not just physically but emotionally and spiritually).

These events, encounters, and the many other happenstances I've had since these events, set me on a path of strengthening my own belief, my own faith, and my own trust in God. It absolutely solidified my conviction that there is a true and living God, that His Word is truth and life, and that through Him, we live, breathe, and have our being! He is a faithful God!

My word from the Lord that He spoke to me; *"If I can raise you from the dead, there is nothing I can't and won't take care of in your life!"*

"For I know the plans I have for you," declares the LORD, "plans to prosper you and not to harm you, plans to give you hope and a future." (Jeremiah 29:11, NIV)

This is my story!

ABOUT ROBIN

Robin Yelverton grew up in Durham, North Carolina, was born and raised in the Lord's Church under the leadership of her father, the late Bishop Frizelle Yelverton, Sr. Having accepted the Lord as her personal savior at a very early age, "Church" became her way of life.

For Robin, growing up as a "PK" (Preacher's Kid) had its own set of challenges as well as serving in the church. Nevertheless, she is grateful to have had the upbringing and training that she received. She has experienced many, many things in church, she believes that there is nothing like having a solid foundation and a rich legacy that has sustained her throughout her life. She wouldn't change that for anything. She has served in many capacities in the church and learned from every area she had the pleasure to serve.

Skilled in the area of administration, Robin worked in the healthcare field for many years of which she is a recent retiree.

She is currently the owner of Robyn's Nest Catering and Wingz and Thingz Food Truck.

Robin has two wonderful children, a daughter, Ceilitia McNair who resides in Charlotte, North Carolina and a son, P. Michael McNair who resides in Greensboro, North Carolina. Connect with Robin at www.facebook.com/robin.yelverton18

ABOUT THE VISIONARY

As an Evangelist, Author, Speaker, and Spiritual Development Coach, Tequita C. Brice inspires women that they have what it takes to live virtuously. She helps women unleash their hidden potential to live, love, and lead their lives by God's design. As a result of working with her, women learn how to live spirit-led lives, strengthen their relationship and commitment to God, and learn how to apply spiritual principles to every area of their lives.

Tequita C. Brice is the CEO of Virtuous Woman Ministries where she builds, strengthens, and empowers women to realize their value, purpose, and worth. Her literary works include her inspiring breakout memoir entitled *FOR MY SHAME: Finding Purpose through Pain* in which she offers encouragement that no matter how perplexing the problem, there is purpose in the process and her highly anticipated *31 Days of Virtue: Awakening the Excellence In You.*

Because her joy and excitement in Christ are contagious, her deep love for her Savior, obvious, and her style of speaking, electric, audiences across the world are drawn to Tequita's message of love, hope, healing and restoration. Though her accomplishments are highlighted, Tequita is an extraordinary woman of virtue whose utmost desire is sincerely to please God. She serves faithfully as an Associate Minister at Monument of Praise Church under the shepherding of Dr. Kevin A. Williams, is the wife of Michael K. Brice and resides near High Point, North Carolina.

Connect with Tequita at www.tequitacbrice.com.

Connect With Us

If you found this book helpful in any way, we would love your feedback. Please leave us a review or feel free to contact any of the authors via the information provided at the end of their stories.

Thank you for your support!
www.churchgirlsbook.com

Every trial, challenge, triumph, and success you've experienced has all been ordained by God. Your life was chosen to be a testimony for others to see the miraculous, transformational power of God. Are you ready to join the C.H.U.R.C.H. Girls Movement and share your story?

Send us an email to author@tequitacbrice.com
with the SUBJECT: Share My Story

www.ingramcontent.com/pod-product-compliance
Lightning Source LLC
Chambersburg PA
CBHW070604010526
44118CB00012B/1446